The troll's body smashes to the floor and you whirl to face the orcs in the doorway.

They draw back, unwilling to attack now they have seen you slay a cave troll with your bare hands. One of them, fatter than the rest and wearing a makeshift iron crown, calls for crossbows. It seems they intend to pepper you with quarrels from the safety of the doorway.

The seneschal calls you to follow him. He is passing his hand up and down the wall behind the throne. 'Quickly, Overlord. The creature is coming back to life.'

Your skin crawls as you see the troll's tattered flesh stretching and crawling across the bones to reknit itself. The wounds are disappearing before your very eyes...

Way of the Tiger
WARBRINGER!

JAMIE THOMSON
& MARK SMITH

FL

Originally published 1986 by Knight Books
This edition published 2014 by Fabled Lands Publishing
an imprint of Fabled Lands LLP

www.sparkfurnace.com

Illustrations by Hokusai, Aude Pfister, Mylène Villeneuve, Sébastien Brunet and Bob Harvey

Edited by Richard S. Hetley

With thanks to Mikaël Louys, Michael Spencelayh, Paul Gresty and David Walters

ISBN-13: 978-1-909905-14-6
ISBN-10: 1909905143

WARNING!

Do not attempt any of the techniques or methods described in this book. They could result in serious injury or death to an untrained user.

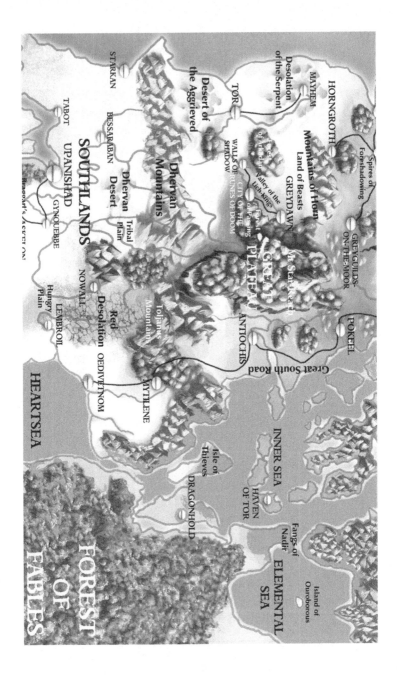

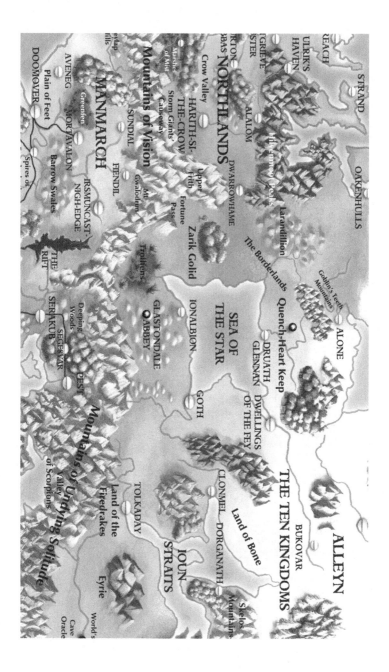

THE WAY OF THE TIGER

Adventure Gamebooks

Ninja Character Sheet

Combat Ratings								
Punch	O							
Kick	O							
Throw	O							
Fate Modifier	O							

Skills	+ Shurikenjutsu

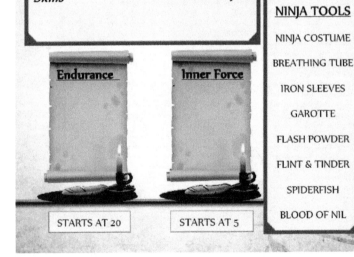

NINJA TOOLS

NINJA COSTUME

BREATHING TUBE

IRON SLEEVES

GAROTTE

FLASH POWDER

FLINT & TINDER

SPIDERFISH

BLOOD OF NIL

Endurance

Inner Force

STARTS AT 20

STARTS AT 5

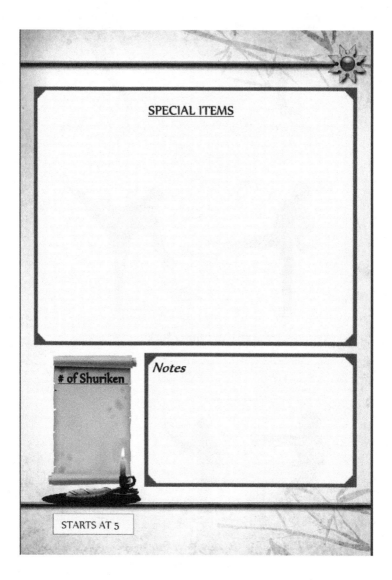

SPECIAL ITEMS

of Shuriken

Notes

STARTS AT 5

Winged Horse Kick

Leaping Tiger Kick

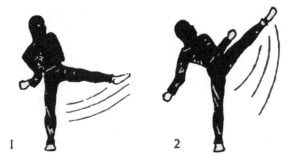

1

2

Forked Lightning Kick

Iron Fist Punch

Tiger's Paw Punch

Cobra Strike Punch

Whirlpool Throw

Dragon's Tail Throw

Teeth of Tiger Throw

THE WAY OF THE TIGER

Adventure Gamebooks

Opponent Encounter Boxes

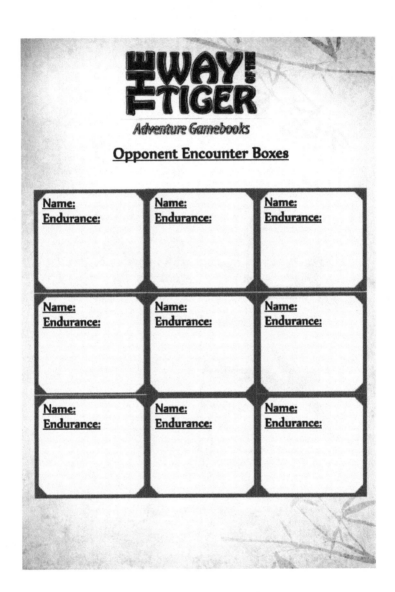

Name: **Endurance:**	**Name:** **Endurance:**	**Name:** **Endurance:**
Name: **Endurance:**	**Name:** **Endurance:**	**Name:** **Endurance:**
Name: **Endurance:**	**Name:** **Endurance:**	**Name:** **Endurance:**

BACKGROUND

On the magical world of Orb, alone in a sea that the people of the Manmarch call Endless, lies the mystical Island of Tranquil Dreams.

Many years have passed since the time when you first saw its golden shores and emerald rice meadows. A servant brought you, braving the distant leagues of the ponderous ocean from lands to which you have never returned. Your loyal servant laid you, an orphan, at the steps of the Temple of the Rock praying that the monks would care for you, for she was frail and dying of a hideous curse.

Monks have lived on the island for centuries, dedicated to the worship of their God, Kwon, He who speaks the Holy Words of Power, Supreme Master of Unarmed Combat. They live only to help others resist the evil that infests the world. Seeing that you were alone and needed care, the monks took you in and you became an acolyte at the Temple of the Rock. Nothing was made of the strange birthmark, shaped like a crown, which you carry on your thigh, though you remember that the old servant insisted that it was of mystical importance. Whenever you have asked about this the monks have bade you meditate and be patient.

The most ancient and powerful of them all, Naijishi, Grandmaster of the Dawn, became your foster-father. He gave you guidance and training in the calm goodness of Kwon, knowledge of men and their ways and how to meditate so that your mind floats free of your body and rides the winds in search of truth.

From the age of six, however, most of your time has been spent learning the Way of the Tiger. Now you are a ninja, a master of the martial arts and a deadly assassin who can kill the most powerful enemies unseen and unsuspected. Like a tiger, you are strong, stealthy, agile, patient in the stalking of prey and deadly. On the Island of Plenty and in the Manmarch the fabled ninja, known as the 'Men with no Shadow', are held in awe – the mere mention of ninja strikes fear into people's hearts. But you are one of the few who worship Kwon and follow the Way of the Tiger. You use your skill as a bringer of death to rid the world of evil-doers.

At an early age you hung by the hands for hours on end from the branches of trees to strengthen your arms. You ran for miles, your light-footed speed enough to keep a thirty-foot ribbon trailing above the ground. You trod tightropes, as agile as a monkey. Now you swim like a fish and leap like a tiger, you move like the whisper of the breeze and glide through the blackest night like a shade. Before he died, Naijishi taught you the Ninja's Covenant.

NINJA NO CHIGIRI

'I will vanish into the night; change my body to wood or stone; sink into the earth and walk through walls and locked doors. I will be killed many times, yet will not die; change my face and become invisible, able to walk among men without being seen.'

It was after your foster-father Naijishi's death that you began to live the words of the Covenant. A man came to the island, Yaemon, Grandmaster of Flame. Using borrowed sorcery he tricked the monks into believing that he was a worshipper of Kwon from the Greater Continent. He was indeed a monk but he worshipped Kwon's twisted brother, Vile, who helps the powerful to subdue the weak, and wicked men to rule fools. Yaemon slew Naijishi – no one could match him in unarmed combat – and he stole the Scrolls of Kettsuin from the Temple. Once more you knew the pain of loss for you had loved Naijishi as a father. You swore an oath to Kwon that one day you would avenge his death… and you *were* avenged. You slew Yaemon and you learned of your ancestry, of the significance of the birthmark carried by the first-born of your family for four generations. Now you are King of the city-state of Irsmuncast.

KING OF IRSMUNCAST

You gathered advisors around you and passed many new laws, some popular, others less than popular, but you managed to govern the city, playing one faction off against another until Irsmuncast came under attack. Not for nothing is the city named Irsmuncast nigh Edge. Its location at the eastern edge of the Manmarch, the lands of men, means that whenever the hosts of evil spew forth from the Bowels of Orb, the great Rift that scores the world like a black pit in a rotten fruit, it is likely that Irsmuncast will be the city they fall upon in their search for new slaves. And so it was early in your reign. The army repulsed them once, but, prompted by your god Kwon the Redeemer, you set out on a quest to recover the Orb and Sceptre which are the traditional emblems of your family's rule. The quest was successful, though it cost you your left eye. Touching the Sceptre transported you magically back to the battlemented tower of the Palace where a terrible sight met your weakened gaze. The city was wreathed in smoke, torched by the evil hordes from the Rift.

As you stared in disbelief a great black raven, ever a bird of ill omen, brought you a message which it dropped from its cruel beak. It was from your old adversary, Honoric, Lord of Doomover and leader of the dread Legion of the Sword of Doom. He once tasted the Blood of Nil at your hands, but, his strong body hardened by the rigours of campaigning, withstood that most potent of poisons. He has sworn revenge and the message which you still hold in your tired hand could hardly be more dire.

'Avenger – an old score shall be settled. The Legion of the Sword of Doom shall conquer the City of Irsmuncast and bring its people into slavery. I swear by Sorcerak to kill you with my own hands – Honoric.'

As Glaivas the Ranger-Lord once told you, the Legion is one of the most feared armies on Orb. The warriors worship the war god, Vasch-Ro, He who sows for the Reaper, and they spread fear about them in battle like a pall.

As things stand you do not even have a city to defend. Your people may all be slaughtered or carried off to the slave pits of the Rift. You must try to regain control of the city at all costs, unless it is already too late.

RULES OF COMBAT

As a master of Taijutsu, the ninja's art of unarmed combat, you have four main ways of fighting: throwing shuriken (see under skills), kicks, punches and throws.

In general it will be harder to hit an opponent when kicking but a kick will do more damage than a punch. A throw, if successful, will allow you to follow up with a possible 'killing blow', but if you fail a throw your Defence against an opponent will be lower, as you are open to attack. Shuriken are a special case and will be mentioned in the text when you can use them.

Whenever you are in a combat you will be asked which type of attack you wish to make. See the Way of the Tiger illustrations for the different types of kicks, punches and throws available to you. Think about your opponent and its likely fighting style. Trying to throw a giant enemy is not going to be as easy as throwing an ordinary man, for example. You will be told which paragraph to turn to, depending on your choice.

When you are resolving combat, you will find it useful to record your opponent's current Endurance score. A number of Encounter Boxes are provided with your Character Sheet for this purpose.

The combats have been presented in such a way that it is possible for you to briefly examine the rules and begin play almost immediately, but fighting is tactical. Do not forget the rules for blocking and Inner Force (see below), as you will rarely be told when to use these in the text.

PUNCH

When you try to strike an enemy with a punch, that enemy will have a Defence number. You need to score higher than this number on the roll of two dice (an Attack Roll). You get to add your Punch Modifier (see below) to this roll. If the score is higher than his or her Defence number, you have punched your opponent successfully. In this case, roll one more die. The result is the amount of damage you have inflicted on your opponent. Every opponent has Endurance or 'hit points'. The damage you do is subtracted from your opponent's Endurance total. If this has reduced your opponent's score to 0 or less, you have won.

Punch Modifier: Whenever you make an Attack Roll to determine whether or not you have successfully punched an opponent, add or subtract your Punch Modifier. This number reflects your skill in using the punches of the Way of the Tiger. Your starting Punch Modifier is 0, as noted on your Character Sheet. This may change during the adventure.

The Enemy's Attack: After you punch, any opponent still in the fight will counter attack. You will be given your Defence number. Roll two dice, and if the score is greater than your Defence, you have been hit. The amount of damage inflicted upon you depends on the opponent and will be noted in the text, in a format such as 'Damage: 1 Die + 1' or '2 Dice' or '1 Die + 2'. Simply roll the required number of dice and add any other number given. This is the total damage inflicted upon you. However, before you subtract this score from your Endurance, you may choose to try and block or parry the attack (see block) to prevent any damage.

KICK

The kick and the Kick Modifier work exactly as the punch, except that a kick will do 2 more points of damage than a punch ('1 Die + 2'). It will often be harder to hit with a kick. If the opponent survives, he or she will counter attack.

THROW

The throw and Throw Modifier work as the punch to determine success. A throw does no damage to your foe; instead, you will be allowed another attack, a punch or kick, with a +2 bonus to hit (like an extra Punch Modifier or Kick Modifier) and +2 to damage. (All bonuses are cumulative – a kick normally does '1 Die + 2' damage, so after a successful throw it does '1 Die + 4'.) The opponent will only counter attack against a throw if you fail.

ENDURANCE

You begin the game with 20 points of Endurance. Keep a running total of your Endurance on your Character Sheet. It will probably be the number that will change most as you are wounded, healed etc. When you reach 0 Endurance or less, you are dead and your adventure ends. When restoring Endurance, you cannot go above your maximum of 20.

BLOCK

As a ninja, a master of Taijutsu, you have the ability to block or parry incoming blows with various parts of your body, often your forearms. For this purpose, thin lightweight iron rods have been sewn into your sleeves enabling you to block even swords and other weapons. During combat, if you have been hit, you may try to block the blow and take no damage. Roll two dice. If the score is less than your Defence given in that combat, you have successfully blocked the blow, and take no damage. If your score is equal to or greater than your Defence, you take damage in the normal way. In any case, because you have taken the time to block, your next attack will be less effective, as your opponent has had more time to react. Whether your block is successful or not, −2 will be applied to your Punch, Kick and Throw Modifier for your next attack only. Remember, you can only block blows, not missiles or magic.

INNER FORCE

You begin the adventure with 5 points of Inner Force. Through meditation and rigorous training you have mastered the ability to unleash spiritual or inner power through your body in the same way as the karate experts of today break blocks of wood and bricks. In any combat, before you roll the dice to determine if you will hit or miss an opponent, you may choose to use Inner Force. If you do, deduct one point from your Inner Force score. This is used up whether or not you succeed in striking your opponent. If you are successful, however, double the damage you inflict – first make your roll for damage and add any bonus (e.g., '1 Die + 2' for a kick), then double the result. When your Inner

Force is reduced to 0, you cannot use Inner Force again until you find some way to restore it – so use it wisely. When restoring Inner Force, you cannot go above your maximum of 5.

FATE

Luck plays its part and the goddess Fate has great power on the world of Orb. Whenever you are asked to make a Fate Roll, roll two dice, adding or subtracting your Fate Modifier. If the score is 7–12, you are lucky and Fate has smiled on you. If the score is 2–6, you are unlucky and Fate has turned her back on you. You begin your adventure with a Fate Modifier of 0. Later on, this might go up or down, as you are blessed or cursed by Fate.

NINJA TOOLS

As well as any equipment you may take depending on your skills (see next), as a ninja you have certain tools with you from the beginning. These are:

THE NINJA COSTUME

During the day you would normally be disguised as a traveller, beggar or suchlike. At night when on a mission, you would wear costume. This consists of a few pieces of black cloth. One piece is worn as a jacket covering the chest and arms, two others are wound around each leg and held in at the waist. Finally, a long piece of cloth is wrapped around the head, leaving only the eyes exposed. The reverse side of the costume can be white, for travel on snowy ground, or green, for travel in woods or grasslands.

IRON SLEEVES
Sewn into the sleeves of your costume are four thin strips of iron, the length of your forearm. These allow you to parry or block blows from swords and other cutting weapons.

BREATHING TUBE
Made from bamboo, this can be used as a snorkel allowing you to remain underwater for long periods of time. It can also be used as a blow-pipe in conjunction with the Poison Needles skill, for added range.

GARROTTE
A specialised killing tool of the ninja, this is a length of wire used to assassinate enemies by strangulation.

FLASH POWDER
This powder, when thrown in any source of flame, causes a blinding flash. You have enough for one use only.

FLINT AND TINDER
Used for making fires.

SPIDERFISH
Salted and cured, this highly venomous fish is used as a source for the deadly poison used in conjunction with the Poison Needles skill, and as a useful way of removing any guardian beasts or animals.

THE BLOOD OF NIL
You also carry one dose of the most virulent poison known on Orb. This venom is extremely difficult and very danger-ous to collect for it is taken from the barb of a scorpion son of the God, Nil, Mouth of the Void. You had used yours long ago, but have found a replacement amongst the bizarre and otherworldly treasures hoarded by the evil Usurper.

THE SKILLS OF THE WAY OF THE TIGER

You have been trained in ninjutsu almost all of your life. Your senses of smell, sight and hearing have been honed to almost superhuman effectiveness. You are well versed in woodcraft, able to track like a bloodhound, and to cover your own tracks. Your knowledge of plants and herb lore enables you to live off the land. You are at the peak of physical fitness, able to run up to 50 miles a day and swim like a fish. Your training included horsemanship, a little ventriloquism, meditation, the ability to hold yourself absolutely still for hours on end, perfecting your balance, and 'The Seven Ways of Going' or disguise. The latter skill involves comprehensive training so that you can perform as a minstrel, for instance, if this disguise is used. However, a major part of this training has been stealth, hiding in shadows, moving silently, and breathing as quietly as possible, enabling you to move about unseen and unheard. You begin the game with these skills.

There are nine other skills. One of these, Shurikenjutsu, is always taught to a ninja in training. This you must take, but you may then choose three other skills from the remaining eight, and note them on your Character Sheet.

SHURIKENJUTSU

You begin the adventure with five shuriken. The type you specialise in are 'throwing stars', small razor-sharp star-shaped disks of metal. You can throw these up to a range of about thirty feet with devastating effect. If you throw a shuriken, you will be given a Defence number for your target. Roll two dice, and if the score is higher than the Defence number, you will have hit your target. The text will describe the damage done. You may find yourself in a position where you are unable to retrieve a shuriken once you have thrown it. Keep a running total in the box provided on your Character Sheet, crossing off a shuriken each time you lose one. If you have none left, you can no longer use this skill. You are free to carry as many as you find in your adventures.

ARROW CUTTING
Requiring excellent muscular co-ordination, hand and eye judgment and reflexes, this skill will enable you to knock aside, or even catch, missiles such as arrows or spears.

ACROBATICS
The ability to leap and jump using flips, cartwheels, etc, like a tumbler or gymnast.

IMMUNITY TO POISONS
This involves taking small doses of virulent poisons over long periods of time, slowly building up the body's resistance. This enables you to survive most poison attempts.

FEIGNING DEATH
Requiring long and arduous training, a ninja with this ability is able to slow down heart rate and metabolism through will power alone, thus appearing to be dead.

ESCAPOLOGY
A ninja with this skill is able to dislocate the joints of the body and to maximise the body's suppleness, allowing movement through small spaces, and escape from bonds and chains by slipping out of them.

POISON NEEDLES
Sometime known as Spitting Needles, with this skill you can place small darts, coated with a powerful poison that acts in the blood stream, onto your tongue. By curling the tongue into an 'O' shape and spitting or blowing, the dart can be propelled up to an effective range of about 15 feet. A useful surprise attack, the source of which is not always perceptible.

PICKING LOCKS, DETECTING AND DISARMING TRAPS
The ability to open locked doors, chests etc. With this skill you would carry various lockpicks in the pockets of your costume, including a small crowbar or jemmy. You are also trained to notice traps and to use the lock-picking tools to disarm them.

CLIMBING

Comprehensive training in the use of a grappling hook and hand and foot clamps, or cat's claws. The padded four-pronged hook has forty feet of rope attached to it. Used to hook over walls, niches etc, allowing you to pull yourself up the rope. The cat's claws are spiked clamps, worn over the palm of the hands and the instep of the feet, enabling you to embed your claws into a wall and climb straight up like a fly, and even to crawl across ceilings.

SPECIAL RULES FOR THIS BOOK

If you have not played and successfully completed Book 4: *OVERLORD!* in the Way of the Tiger series then you begin this book with the equipment and skills listed. If you have successfully completed Book 4 then you should continue with the same character. Simply transfer all the information on your original Character Sheet to the one given here. You will carry five shuriken again and your Endurance and Inner Force will have been restored, though if you were tainted by the sorcery of an Amulet of Nullaq then you have a maximum of only 4 points of Inner Force. You also continue Book 5 with any special items you may have picked up in your adventures and do not forget to transfer all your Punch, Kick, etc, Modifiers to your new Character Sheet.

While adventuring in Book 3: *USURPER!* you may also have learnt just one of the following two superior skills, taught by the Grandmaster of the Dawn at the Temple of the Rock:

SHINREN

Or the Training of the Heart. ShinRen is a secret knowledge passed on during several weeks in the hills of the Island of Tranquil Dreams. You have learned iron control of your emotions; you can walk over glowing coals without turning a hair, endure heat, cold, wind, rain, hunger, thirst and pain that would send a normal person mad. Your instincts have been honed so that you may 'read' any person like an open book – having learnt the language that the body talks, understanding what people think by observing their mannerisms and the way they breathe, the roving of their eyes and their stance. You are able to understand a complicated situation at a glance and act, seizing any opening and taking any chance that appears.

YUBI-JUTSU

Or Nerve-Striking. You have learnt how to maim and kill with even quite light blows to vital nerve centres – a technique especially useful when beset by many adversaries at once, or against a formidable human foe. You know the anatomy of man in fine detail, the unprotected points and nerve centres where an accurate blow can stun or even kill.

When you are ready to begin the adventure, turn to **1**.

1

The smoke from the burning city obscures the scene. It is difficult to make anything out from your lofty vantage point at the top of the Palace. There is no sign of Force-Lady Gwyneth nor of the Irsmuncast army. You have no way of knowing whether all resistance has been crushed or whether there is still hope of turning the tide. The Orb and Sceptre are heavy in your hands. You have no idea whether they hold potent magic that will aid you or whether they are mere baubles, no more than the symbols of the overlordship which you have lost. Will you descend the staircase into the Palace (turn to **57**) or examine the Orb and Sceptre on the battlements (turn to **45**)?

2

You ride on, ahead of your troops. Soon you come to the valley, where your scouts reported a sighting of Honoric's army. You continue up it, following a winding river, the River of Beasts, that flows through the valley. You pass by a village on the left as you leap a small stream. As dusk falls, a manor house appears ahead. It seems deserted, and as you rein in your horse you see the reason why. A half-mile beyond, a great army is settling down for the night's camp. The rosy glow of the setting sun seems to set aflame the gleaming steel of fifteen thousand spears, and the sound of many men bivouacking fills the evening air. As you watch, your spirit sinks at the sight of such a mighty army. You recognise banners not only of Doomover but of the cities of Aveneg, Horngroth, Mortavalon and others. Honoric has been hard at work – a powerful alliance of cities is ranged against you. You must try to learn more. Turn to **12**.

3

You meet no further resistance, casually almost knocking aside two Orcs left behind in the stampede, until you reach the steps to the great gateway of the Palace itself. Unfortunately one of the orcish chieftains, using the foulest language you have ever heard, curses his Orcs for cowards and rallies them. Even more ominously for you, he has called up reinforcements, a company of Orcs armed with crossbows. Will you risk a feigned attack, instead leaping high above their heads and vanishing into smoke-filled Palace Road (turn to **107**) or hold up the Sceptre and command the Orcs to bow down to the rightful Overlord of Irsmuncast (turn to **95**)?

4

You invite suggestions from your commanders. Refer to the map at **342** as needed.

Gwyneth suggests a defensive formation with a refused left flank. 'The right flank should rest on the Wickerwood, with Gliftel's Elves in the wood itself. Four hundred warriors of Béatan should occupy the Old Farm, with some cavalry positioned on Colwyn's Mound, and then a line of units stretching to the Greenridge, with the centre resting in Hartwig Fell's Farm. Antocidas and his mercenaries should be held in reserve on Tallhill, where the Overlord Avenger's command post should be. Finally, I would suggest Glaivas and his Rangers should wait in ambush at the Old Bridge to hold it for as long as possible should any try to cross it.'

'No, I disagree,' says Obuda Varhegyen, his voice heavily accented. 'We should use the terrain to our best advantage in setting up a defensible position. Swordsmistress Hivatala should march now to hold Ruric's Bridge with her cavalry close behind to plug any gaps should the enemy show signs of breaking through and to provide an attack capability. The troops under Ba'al should hold the ford, while Gliftel's bowmen occupy Woodnugget Wood. Gwyneth's troops and those of Antocidas can hold the ditch from Woodnugget Wood to the Wickerwood, with her cavalry close behind near Colwyn's Mound. A thousand men could be held in reserve along with Glaivas' Rangers, who can be used to plug any gaps. Finally, I would suggest that the Overlord Avenger sets up his command post on the Greenridge. That is my counsel. Thank you.'

Turn to **410**.

5

Summoning your knowledge of the ways of the mind and body, the ancient teachings of the monks of the Island of Tranquil Dreams, you sink into a trance that is like a deep hibernation. The spiders crawl all over you. You are dimly aware of it, but they will not use their poison fangs on an animal they sense is dead. The Dark Elves have no such qualms, however, and one runs you through with a stabbing sword before you can come back out of your trance. Now Honoric and the forces from the Rift will carve out the fate of Irsmuncast between them.

6

The Old One lies at your horse's feet. You look around to see that the Doomover Levies are in full flight, routing off the field of battle. Your warriors are shouting with joy. The cavalry and the women of Horngroth have been forced to retreat, but you can see them slowly regrouping some way off, readying to renew the fight, albeit depleted. To your dismay, you can see to the left that the three thousand strong group of soldiers from Aveneg, Mortavalon and the Spires are now close to the Greenridge, from where they can swing around into the rear of the defenders there, Antocidas' mercenaries and the men of Serakub. The battle hangs in the balance. Will you lead your cavalry in a charge against the forces that are regrouping ahead of you, the cavalry and the women of Horngroth, and send the Warrior Women of Dama marching as quickly as possible to the Greenridge (turn to **196**) or lead your cavalry as fast as possible to the Greenridge and split the footsoldiers of Dama, leaving those of Serakub where they are and commanding those of Irsmuncast to follow you (turn to **206**)?

7

You look around. The pressure is still on. The far left with the women of Serakub at Ruric's Bridge seems secure enough. The soldiers at the ford are still grimly holding on, although they seem depleted by a third. But the sight at Woodnugget Wood fills you with trepidation. The monks of the Scarlet Mantis have appeared again and are running into the wood. The Elves can no longer keep up a steady volley of arrows at the flank of the Legion, but must now be fighting for their lives. The situation at the farm has become desperate. The Legion is repeatedly moving back to allow their crossbowmen to open fire before they charge back into the fray, and they are now applying heavy pressure all along the line from the farm to the wood. Not only that, but Honoric's cavalry has regrouped and, although it is only half as strong, is readying itself for another charge. The battle is in the balance.

Will you lead your cavalry in a desperate attempt to rout the attackers at the ford as quickly as you can (turn to **268**), order a general fighting withdrawal to Bridgebeam (turn to **258**) or ask Glaivas and his twenty Rangers, experts in woodcraft, to circle Woodnugget Wood as fast as they can and attack the monks of the Scarlet Mantis in the rear (turn to **278**)?

8

Before you can finish, a cry goes up from the Doomover line and a small group of cavalrymen – members of the élite Bringers of Doom – gallops forwards amid roars of approval and cries of rage from both armies. The cavalrymen ride towards you. Those of your own troops nearest to you cry, 'Back, my lord, back!' and you are forced to retire. The cavalrymen sweep up Honoric, who, though barely alive, is cursing them loudly for besmirching his honour. You make your way through the ranks of your cheering soldiers to your command post, where some Healers of Avatar are waiting to tend you. A similar situation must be occurring on the other side of the stream, for it is not until the priestesses have used their magic to restore up to 10 points of any Endurance you may have lost that battle is joined. If your allies are the men of the Spires of Foreshadowing and of Fiendil, turn to **74**. If they are of Serakub and Aveneg, turn to **84**.

9

He nods as if he believes you and then, as quick as a flash, rips off the eye-patch that is part of your disguise. Your face, adorned as it is, cannot be forgotten by a trained assassin. He bids you begone, and you find that all your attempts to see Dom the Prescient henceforth are thwarted, for his defenders will not believe that an Overlord would pretend to be a kitchen scullion. When Honoric's wrath breaks across Irsmuncast, your forces are terribly outnumbered. You die defending the walls and Irsmuncast is taken.

10

You can see that Doré le Jeune is angered by your order, but he keeps himself in check and your men hold their position. Then a trumpet blast sounds. The legion on the near side of the ford, in order now, launch an attack at the men in and around the farm – a bitter, vicious fight begins there, but for the moment your left flank is holding its own with good support from the elfin bows. Then the crossbowmen, the Rain of Doom, advance, followed by the massed allies of Honoric. They halt and open fire on your cavalry. The range is long and casualties light. Doré le Jeune looks up at you expectantly. If you tried to spy out Honoric's camp last night and found out the contents of three large wooden boxes, turn to **180**. If you do not know what the boxes contain, turn to **190**.

11

Three days after your great victory, the fires have been extinguished and the city is returning to some semblance of order. The mood of the people veers hysterically between despair and joy at being alive. Few families have not suffered the loss of a dear one, but all know that their fate under the rule of Shadazar would have been unthinkably black. The task of repairing the breaches in the city wall is begun immediately, and the laws that you enacted before your journey to seek the Orb and Sceptre are in force once again. Gwyneth's troops are maintaining order. You have become entirely dependent upon her in the times of dire extremity, but she is busy re-forming an army and overseeing the repair of Irsmuncast's fortifications. If you are wounded, restore your Endurance to 20 from the ministrations of the Healers of Avatar – Greystaff himself lays the Hands of Excellent Health spell on you. If you have a Purple Jade Ring, turn to **55**. If not, turn to **21**.

12

You decide to wait until night has fallen before stealing into the camp. There you can 'procure' the uniform of one of the soldiers and wander around with impunity. There is much to be learnt from camp fire gossip, as well as the class and number of troops you will be facing in battle.

Night falls and heavy clouds obscure the moon; ideal weather for one such as you. You steal forwards unseen and unheard, pleased to exercise after so long those skills at which you excel. You come to the camp's outposts, a circle of pickets. Ahead of you two guards, with spears and chainmail surcoats, stand warming themselves around a small fire. You crouch at the edge of the firelight. If you act quickly enough, you may be able to disable both without being spotted. Will you creep up behind them, throw some flash powder on the fire and then attack (turn to **22**), creep forwards and use Poison Needles, if you have that skill (turn to **32**), hurl a shuriken at one (turn to **42**) or creep up behind them and attack from behind (turn to **52**)?

13

A crack, unnoticed over the years, runs around the raised square of marble. Tapping the marble, you find a hollow recess behind it. There is also a slight staining of the marble as if caused by some noxious substance. Warning the Seneschal to keep back, you press the top of the square, holding a piece of drapery as a shield as the marble square revolves. There is the sound of shattering glass, and a spray of acid burns through the drapery although you are unharmed. Turn to **111**.

14

Gwyneth smiles. 'Victory may yet be ours, Overlord,' she says, and she rides away to organise the disposition of the troops.

Doré le Jeune and the White Mage decide to stay with you on Tallhill, to await events before committing themselves. So do Hengist and his comrades. As your men move into position, so Honoric reacts. His dispositions are shown on

the map opposite. Note this paragraph number down as a record of your strategy and so that you can refer to the map when the battle begins. Turn to **388**.

15

Cautiously you advance on one of the spiders, which scurries quickly towards you across the burnt earth, zigzagging erratically and gravitating towards cracks in the earth and stones as if seeking shelter. You bend to pick up a piece of dead wood with which to flatten it, but as you do so the nearest Dark Elf sorcerer speaks a Spell of Immolation and the wood bursts into flames and just as quickly crumbles into a pile of useless ash. You retreat, hoping that the paths of the other two spiders, which you have lost sight of, will have crossed, for if they meet, you remember in a flash of inspiration, female executioner spiders will fight to the death. Will you retreat to the tree and climb it (turn to **413**) or fall back further towards the pier of rock (turn to **205**)?

16

The Old One lies at your horse's feet. You look up from your struggle to a glorious sight. The opposing cavalry has been driven off and is in retreat, falling back in good order. Your presence and the presence of Doré le Jeune, who fights like a whirlwind, was enough to give your soldiers the edge over the élite Bringers of Doom. But casualties have been heavy on both sides. Will you pursue Honoric's cavalry with your own (turn to **356**) or swing around to attack the Legion in the rear (turn to **366**)?

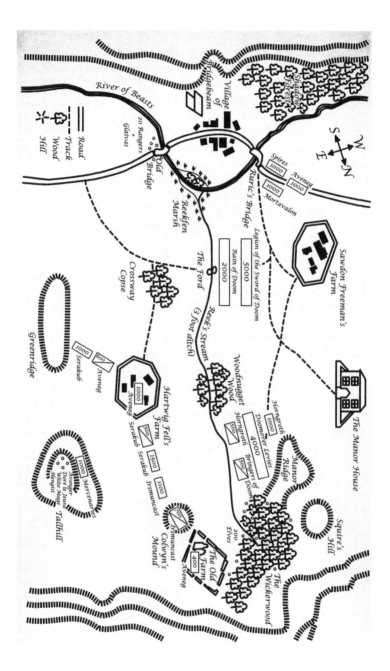

You decide to tell them no more than that you are travelling to Serakub and they lend you a reserve mount. Many are curious about your glowing green Orb of an eye, but they suppress their curiosity when you pretend that you are sensitive about it. You learn much on the journey. There is no one ruler of Serakub; it is a republic. A hundred Prodromese, each chosen by the vote of the populace, sit in a council called the Boule where decisions of state are made. The followers of Béatan hold a few votes more than either Dama or the nature god's followers. It seems you will have to make a speech before them all.

The City of Serakub lies on the banks of the beautiful blue waters of the Ebune river amid richly fertile fields. Everywhere flowers blossom and there are clouds of many-hued butterflies in the meadows. You are escorted through the city gates into the beautiful City of Gardens. Many of the buildings of the city have been built out of many different types of stone of many colours. Most are covered in a drapery of flowering creepers, clematis, Ra's glory, red ivy and widowfoil. You are taken to the city hall in which is the Hall of Governance where the Boule meets. Scribes fire a number of questions at you, writing all the time with ostentatious flourishes of their quills. Their version of the common tongue is at first difficult to understand, but with practice this improves. At length you are called upon to address the Boule. Turn to **67**.

18

Refer to the map at paragraph **14** for the disposition of forces. You can make notes on the map at **342** if necessary.

Trumpets blare harshly, and shouted orders echo on the breeze to you from Honoric's lines. The troops near Ruric's Bridge begin to cross it, headed for the Old Bridge, where you hope Glaivas can hold them up for a time. The Legion of the Sword of Doom begins crossing the ford. When the Legion begins to march around Crossway Copse, Honoric's cavalry and the Doomover Levies charge forwards, the hoofbeats of the cavalry drumming like thunder as they hurtle onwards.

Turn to **106**.

19

The Troll's body smashes to the floor and you whirl to face the spectating Orcs. They blench and almost fall over themselves in their haste to get out of your way. They fear to chance their arms against a Troll-slayer. The grey warty skin of the Troll ripples unnaturally and your own skin crawls as the Troll's oozes slowly over the bared bones to reknit, leaving ugly purplish blotches where once the flesh was rent. The Troll will soon have recovered, so you decide to pursue the Orcs, hoping to escape the Palace before they are rallied by some other powerful denizen of the Rift. If you used a shuriken in your battle, you must leave it behind. Turn to **3**.

20

As the men of the Spires retire to the stream they begin to fall into disarray, losing their footing in the ditch. The enemy is almost upon them, and your heart leaps as it looks as if the men will be swept away under the onslaught. But miraculously they just manage to regain their formation when their attackers reach the ditch. Battle is joined, and the clash of weapons and the cries of the wounded fill the air – but your men are holding, just. Desperately you canter off to meet the now decimated cavalry, which is set to flee off the field. On the far left, the Legion of the Sword of Doom and its cavalry are charging the defenders at the farm repeatedly.

The fighting is desperate, but your men look strong enough to hold on for a little longer.

Towards you come the fleeing horsemen, some thousand left. You rein in your horse and raise your Sceptre high, calling on the power of the Sceptre, your false eye glowing with light. 'To me, warriors, to me. I can lead you to victory!' you cry. If you refused the challenge with Honoric before the battle, turn to **40**. If you accepted, turn to **50**.

<h2 style="text-align:center">21</h2>

Of the city notables who had been so influential when you cast down the Usurper, four are either dead or flown. Parsifal, the head of the monastery of your god Kwon, was assassinated by Mandrake, the Guildmaster of Assassins from far away Wargrave Abbas. He has been replaced by Hengist, a younger man who is a dangerous martial artist. Together you have already begun to retrain your fellow monks so that the martial arts tradition of the Temple to Kwon in Irsmuncast should be worthy of its name. The Lord High Steward, once the Usurper's instrument of subjugation, is dead, and word is that he met his end struggling for power with Shadazar herself. Foxglove, latterly the shrewd and captivating head of the Order of the Yellow Lotus, the secret informers, has disappeared without trace, though the rumour is that she betrayed Irsmuncast by revealing to the Dark Elves the weaknesses of the city's defences. Whatever the truth, her Order is no more. Golspiel and the other merchants are long departed from the city. You must look to trade if the city is to feed itself. The other notables, the rabble-rousing Demagogue, Gwyneth, Greystaff and Solstice, the High Priest of the inscrutable Templars to Time, have all survived. Turn to **31**.

22

You glide up silently behind the guards and then dart forwards, throwing the powder on the fire before they can react (cross it from your Character Sheet). You shut your eyes as a great blaze of white light splits the night. The two guards stagger about blindly. You strike one down, but the other cries out in alarm. The flash of light has already alerted other pickets – shouts and the sound of many running feet come to you on the night breeze. They will be upon you in a moment. Will you give up your attempt to spy at Honoric's camp (turn to **62**) or continue with your mission (turn to **72**)?

23

Shadazar realises too late what you are doing. As she races for the castellated top of the Temple to Dama on Cross Street so that she can regain her natural form, you plummet down from above her and break her back with the force of your swoop. The dragon-vulture body falls to the street and resumes the true form of the Dark Elf Shadazar. She is quite dead. There is a moan from the forces of evil, who break and run towards the city gates as you soar above them. You fly down to the Palace gardens just in time, as the potion wears off and you resume natural form as if you had planned it. There is a great cheer from the people. You have delivered the city from evil, and the popularity of your rule is assured if you govern wisely. Turn to **11**.

24

Obuda Varhegyen nods with grim satisfaction. 'So shall the blade of Honoric be blunted on the shield of our defence,' says Ba'al portentously.

Doré le Jeune and the White Mage decide to stay with you on the Greenridge to await events before committing themselves. So do Hengist and his comrades. As your men move into position, so Honoric reacts. His dispositions are shown on the map opposite. Note this paragraph number down as a record of your strategy and so that you can refer to the map when the battle begins. Turn to **388**.

25

As you advance along the Avenue of Seasons, a group of Orcs flees before you to bring the news of your impending attack to the forces concentrated around the Palace. At the corner of Belfry Street a man you recognise as Radziwil, one of the members of Foxglove's Order of the Yellow Lotus, once the Usurper's secret informers, asks to speak to you. You beckon him forward, but Gwyneth draws her sword and moves her horse between the two of you. 'You can speak your message to me, slime-worm.' Radziwil looks offended. His mock courtesy as he defers to the Force-Lady jars horribly with the death and extremity of human suffering all around you. 'If you attack now, Force-Lady, you will retake the city. The Orcs have found the Palace wine cellars and are too busy looting to fight.' Gwyneth motions him away and then confides: 'Foxglove deserted us. She told the Dark Elves where to undermine the city wall to gain access to the sewers. Thanks to her and the Yellow Lotus we were taken by surprise.' Will you attack as Radziwil suggests (turn to **417**) or take a path through the part of the city which has not yet fallen and try to link up with Antocidas and the mercenaries (turn to **405**)?

26

However, after you have issued the order, nothing happens. A runner appears from the mercenaries. Breathlessly, and not without a trace of guilt, he says, 'Ah, Overlord, Antocidas

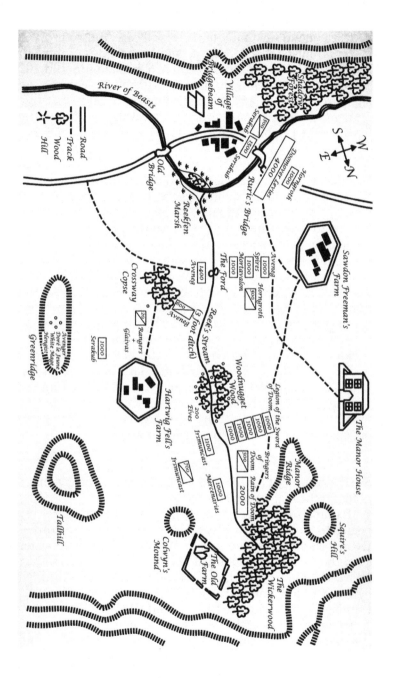

instructs me to say that... um... he will carry out your order if you promise to... er... pay us another talent on return to Irsmuncast.' A talent is the weight of a man in pure gold, the currency with which a city is run. Will you stifle your rage and agree (turn to **36**) or refuse outright in disgust at this outrageous demand and order your cavalry to charge the flanks of the Legion of the Sword of Doom (turn to **368**)?

27

You decide to use your Sceptre as a staff on your journey. You come to realise it special power, where just by wishing to, you can influence people who are not already hostile to you. The first leg of your journey takes you obliquely past the southern tip of the Rift, the Bowels of Orb, that great chasm like a rotting seam on the fruit that is Orb. In the caverns and catacombs that riddle its cliffs and descend to the centre of Orb dwells so much evil that the minds of men cannot even begin to comprehend. Somewhere far from the light of day lurk the cities of the Old Ones and others from the age before the coming of man. You decide to give the chasm a wide berth, but your eagle eyes notice a minute black speck circling far above you in the clear sky. It is joined by a mate, and you can guess from the patterns that they fly that they are carrion crows, as like as not sent to spy on you by Dark Elves from the Rift. You press on, anxious not to waste time. Turn to **243**.

28

See the map at **34** for the disposition of forces. You can make notes on the map at **342** if necessary.

Trumpets bray, orders are bellowed and Honoric's army begins to move. The cavalry and the Legion of the Sword of Doom begin to cross the stream. When they are on the other side, the cavalry gives a great shout and charges forwards, hooves drumming like thunder, heading straight for the men between Tallhill and Hartwig Fell's Farm, the crossbowmen running behind, with the Legion itself following up.

Honoric's allies at the ford also charge forwards but meet staunch resistance from the Warrior Women of Serakub and a bitter mêlée ensues. On the far left, the Doomover Levies stream across the bridge, but in the confined space Gwyneth's soldiers are cutting them down in droves. Some Levies try to run or refuse to charge, but behind them the soldiers of Horngroth are slaying any who refuse to obey orders.

Your Corps of Bannermen, twenty standard-bearers with banners particular to individual units, stand ready to signal your orders. Will you order your cavalry to charge forwards and meet Honoric's cavalry (turn to **236**) or send your four hundred reserves quickly to reinforce the men between the farm and Tallhill (turn to **246**)?

29

You had expected to see a man whose brow was lined with wisdom, a man with charisma redolent of great power, yet when you come face to face with Dom you are surprised that you were completely wrong. He is short and quite powerfully built, yet obviously no fighting man. He wears a magnificent robe of many colours, but he is only in early middle age and his eyes twinkle merrily beneath a forehead unlined by cares. He sits on a throne that is carved from rocks, of as many colours as his robe, somehow welded together. The effect is of a colourful waterfall of glass. 'Avenger, you come to seek an alliance against that braggart Honoric whom you have upset so deeply. You haven't much time. The Spawn of the Rift still covet your city, Overlord.' He doesn't stand on ceremony and he has the air of one who knows everything there is to know about the matter at hand. Turn to **39**.

30

As the men of the Spires reach the ditch, the allies of Honoric charge. Your men are flung back in disarray and, losing their footing in the ditch, their formation begins to break up. To your horror, within moments they have been swept away, and the enemy comes pouring through. Suddenly the monks of the Scarlet Mantis burst out of the Old Farm, where they had crept, unheard, from the Wickerwood and assault Colwyn's Mound. There are two hundred of them, and all your nearest troops are routed. You put up a strong defence, but it is not long before you are overwhelmed and slain.

31

The first audience that you give in the Throne Room this morning is to Force-Lady Gwyneth, captain of the Watch and general of what remains of the army. Attired in well-worn armour as always, she strides purposefully towards the throne and bows low. You have never seen her without martial accoutrements, you realise, even at royal banquets. She presses you to abandon the normal form of government through your advisors and the council of Star Chamber. You reply that you will govern just as your father governed and that the council must be reconvened. Just then the court chamberlain announces that a messenger has arrived. 'He says he has come from the cities of the Spires of Foreshadowing and... er... Doomover, Overlord. He looks no more than a strolling player. Shall I call the scribe?' Gwyneth raises her eyebrows at the mention of the City of Doomover and you bid the court chamberlain show the stranger into your presence. Turn to **81**.

32

The needle is on your tongue and hurtling towards the target in an instant. Your aim is perfect. It catches the guard behind the knee, where there is no armour. He twitches and falls dead in moments. The other guard turns in surprise and, unsure as to what has afflicted his comrade, kneels over him with his back to you. Instantly you leap forwards and deliver a crushing blow to the back of his neck, knocking him out. Hurriedly you don the armour and surcoat of one of the guards. You are now dressed as a swordsman of Vasch-Ro from the legion of the City of Aveneg. Turn to **122**.

33

In the centre of the Square of the Seasons is Force-Lady Gwyneth, swordswoman par excellence and High Priestess at the Temple to Dama, Shieldmaiden of the Gods. Clustered around her, holding aloft flaming torches, are about two hundred of her soldiers, mostly heavily armoured swordswomen, some, like her, still on horseback. Townsfolk too are there, and what looks like the remnants of a city militia, led by the fanatical Demagogue who even now exhorts them to fight on, 'For to surrender is to die'. Greystaff too, the High Priest of the Temple to Avatar the One, the Supreme Principle of Good, is there with perhaps a score of his priesthood, who are using their healing magicks on the shieldmaidens.

Gwyneth calls for silence and you choose this moment to descend to the paving of the square and go among your people once again. There is a resounding cheer when you are recognised. Your miraculous appearance seems to have given them new hope. Gwyneth tells you that scattered pockets of resistance still remain. The mercenaries under Antocidas the One-Eyed have refused to throw their lot in with the Spawn of the Rift and still hold the barracks. Gwyneth has retreated to the Temple to Time to plead with the priests to use their potent spellcraft in the fight against evil. But the doors to the Snowfather's Temple remain barred. Her overtures have been rebuffed.

Now you must plan with her a strategy for hitting back against the forces of evil who, feeling the battle is already won, have become scattered and fallen to looting. The enemy is concentrated around the Palace under the command of Shadazar, whose infamous deeds have made her one of the few dwellers in the Rift to be known by name. Will you march down the Avenue of Seasons and give battle in Palace Road (turn to **25**) or take a route through the part of the city which has not yet fallen and try to unite with Antocidas the One-Eyed (turn to **37**)?

34

Hivatala nods quietly to herself and rides away to oversee the disposition of forces.

Doré le Jeune and the White Mage decide to stay with you on the Greenridge to await events before committing themselves. So do Hengist and his comrades. As your men move into position, so Honoric reacts. His dispositions are shown on the map opposite. Note this paragraph number down as a record of your strategy and so that you can refer to the map when the battle begins. Turn to **388**.

35

Your last throwing star has ricocheted far away and you have not killed the executioner spiders. Two jump on you at once. You bat them off feverishly, but it is too late. Tiny fangs have broken your skin and the poison courses through your veins. It will take only seconds to die. Now Irsmuncast will be fought over by Honoric and the forces from the Rift.

36

The runner races away. Antocidas' mercenaries charge forwards. The crossbowmen fire a volley, but the mercenaries, veterans all, pull up short and crouch behind their shields minimising casualties before charging home to devastating effect. The crossbowmen scatter and run as Antocidas leads his mercenaries on into the flank of the Legion of the Sword of Doom. However, elements of the Legion manage to turn to face and receive their charge. The rest of the crossbowmen begin to move into a position to assault the flank of the mercenaries with a counter attack. Looking up, you see that the White Mage has slain all the Wyverns, but his robes are crimson with blood. It is all he can do to reach the ground safely.

The battle hangs in the balance. All you have left uncommitted are the five hundred cavalry of the Spires on Colwyn's Mound. Will you order them to charge forwards, swing right around Antocidas' mercenaries into the crossbowmen and then, with luck, on to the rear of the Legion (turn to **46**) or will you leave Tallhill and, with Doré le Jeune, lead the charge personally (turn to **56**)?

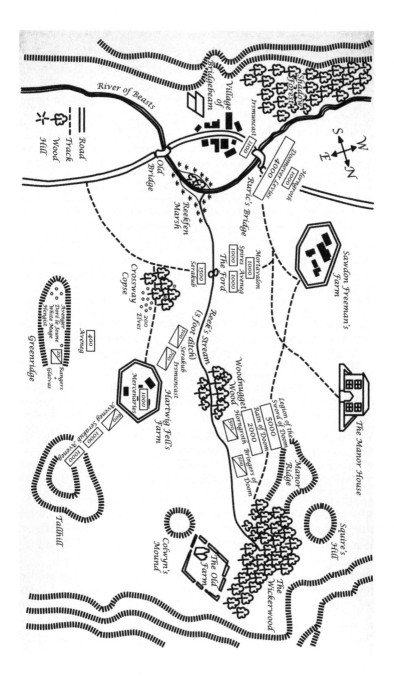

River of Beasts

Village of Bridgebeam

Shadow Forest

S W N E

Irminmast 1100

Doomslayers 1000

Old Bridge

Reekfen Marsh

Ruric's Bridge

Sawdon Freeman's Farm

Road
Track
Wood
Hill

Mortavalon 1000
Spires Aveneg 1000
1000

Serakub 1500
The Ford

Crossway Copse

Serakub 200 Elves

Reefe's Stream (3 foot ditch)

Serakub 500
Irminmast 500

Woodnugget Wood

The Manor House

Avenar Dor le Jeune White Mage Hengist
Rangers + Glaivas 20
400 Avenar

Greenridge

Mercenaries 1000

Hartwig Fell's Farm

Legion of the Sword of Doom
Horngroth 500
Ram of Doom 2000
5000
Bringers of Doom 500

Manor Ridge

Squire's Hill

Tallhill

Avenag Serakub Avenag
1000 1000
600 Avenag

Colwyn's Mound

The Old Farm

The Wickerwood

37

Seeing that there are still some whose resistance is not broken, many more of the townsfolk rally to the Sceptre as you march towards the barracks, until by the time you sight the banner of Antocidas, the golden sword and bulging money-bag, you have a force nigh on a thousand strong. Antocidas has defended the barracks cunningly, losing few men, but the mercenaries are ringed about with foes far outnumbering your combined forces. The bugler sounds the attack and the call is answered from the barracks. Between you and Antocidas is an army of Orcs, but they are led by a company of Dark Elves, tall, lithe and graceful, almost too beautiful to be evil, but cankered of heart, shunned by all others of their race. The charge is led by the swordswomen. Will you join them in the vanguard and attack the Dark Elves (turn to **289**) or hang back and watch (turn to **297**)?

38

Refer to the map at paragraph **24** for the disposition of troops. You can make notes on the map at **342** if you wish.

Trumpets blare harshly and orders are shouted. The battle begins. Immediately Honoric's crossbowmen, the Rain of Doom, run forwards and two thousand crossbow bolts fly at Antocidas' mercenaries. The Legion of the Sword of Doom advances to the ditch to engage Gwyneth's warriors, while the Bringers of Doom charge. A great battle cry goes up as the attack begins.

Simultaneously Honoric's allies also begin a full-blooded assault on the men of Aveneg defending the ford but the Levies on the far left make no attempt to take Ruric's Bridge. The Legion of the Sword of Doom and the cavalry become disordered as they try to cross the ditch, and their attack loses impetus, enabling Gwyneth's warriors to inflict many casualties as their attackers reach them almost in dribs and drabs. But then the monks of the Scarlet Mantis suddenly burst out of the Wickerwood to fall on the flanks of Antocidas' mercenaries with devastating effect. Under the deadly rain of bolts, the cavalry attack and the crippling flank attack, the mercenaries, having lost over a third of their men within a few minutes, just break and run. Fleeing for their lives, they stream past Gwyneth's cavalry. Turn to **48**.

39

Still you have not spoken as he asks you: 'Did you know, Avenger, that if I were to grant you aid the City of Mortavalon would ally with Honoric? You would face not only the Legion of the Sword of Doom but also the Legion of the Angel of Death and the élite heavy cavalry, the Wings of Death.' Will you say that you know you will be victorious if Dom becomes your ally (turn to **59**) or ask him how it is that he knows so much (turn to **69**)?

40

The cavalry streams past you, ignoring you completely. Their fear and their lack of confidence in you are such that not even the Sceptre can affect them. Disconsolately you return to Colwyn's Mound. Then the monks of the Scarlet Mantis burst out of the Old Farm, where they had crept unheard from the Wickerwood, and assault Colwyn's Mound. There are two hundred of them, and all your nearest troops are routed. You put up a strong defence, but it is not long before you are overwhelmed and slain.

41

You smash your beak against the dragon-vulture again and again, all the time raking her body savagely with your claws, but Shadazar wraps her tail around you and bears you down, still struggling, to the ground, where, helped by her minions, she finishes you off. Shadazar will be victorious and the eastern end of the Manmarch is lost to man.

42

As quickly as a striking snake you send a throwing star hurtling towards the nearest guard. Make an Attack Roll. You must roll higher than a 7 since it is dark. If you succeed, turn to **82**. If you miss, turn to **92**.

43

Wargrave Abbas is a coastal city far to the north, with a strong military tradition. The Temple to Dama runs an academy where would-be mercenaries are taught the arts of war. The most powerful soldier there is a woman called Alfrida Watchguard. You spent time there on your return journey to the Island of Tranquil Dreams from Quench-heart Keep, finding both sanctuary and danger in the Temple to Kwon, as there you were first pursued by Mandrake, their Guildmaster of Assassins. It is at least a month's journey to Wargrave, and most unlikely that you could return from there with an army long before the first of Grimweird.

Return to **61**.

44

Before the council breaks up fully you tell them of the Wyverns that Honoric will be using in battle. Everyone looks crestfallen until the White Mage says, 'I shall deal with these creatures myself, and with he who controls them, or die trying, Overlord. As soon as battle commences I will seek them out and keep them at bay, using all the arcane arts I know, no doubt.'

Gravely you thank him, marvelling at the strength and determination of your friends and allies.

Turn to **54**.

45

The Sceptre bears the hippogriff insignia of your family, but neither it nor the Orb bears any inscription nor any obvious means of activation. It would take a powerful magician to unravel their secrets for you, if indeed they hold any. The emerald Orb is about the right size and shape to fit into the hollow eye socket where your left eye once was, the eye you lost battling the Grandmaster of Shadows in the Mountains of Undying Solitude.

If you would like to try and fit the green Orb into the socket, turn to **123**. If not, turn to **135**.

46

The cavalry canters off the Mound and charges forwards. But it suffers heavy losses from the rest of Honoric's crossbowmen, and although these give way the cavalry charge is largely ineffectual.

Finally, the men of the Spires break and run, and the Legion of the Sword of Doom and the remaining cavalry pour through, wheeling around to roll up the rest of your army. Soon it is a full rout. You are caught in the open, trying to rally your forces, by a squadron of the Bringers of Doom, and cut down almost in passing. But, perhaps, you will be remembered in a song.

47

You swoop and turn, waiting until you have the chance to attack without being caught by the dragon-vulture's barbed tail. At last you can strike, but as your beak closes around Shadazar's neck the effects of the potion wear off and you resume your normal form. You are left hanging by your teeth from the scaly neck. With a threshing twist of her body, Shadazar throws you off and you fall to the street below. Lose 10 Endurance. If you are still alive, Shadazar believes you dead. It is only the depth of horse droppings and mud into which you have fallen that has saved you. Turn to **113**.

48

Dismayed, you are about to order your Corps of Bannermen, twenty standard-bearers with banners particular to various units, to signal the cavalry of Irsmuncast to charge when the full force of the Legion hits the outnumbered infantry at the stream. The crossbowmen have wheeled around, poised to unleash a deadly volley into the flank, when Force-Lady Gwyneth, fighting alongside her troops, orders a fighting retreat – she had no choice other than to face swift annihilation.

Desperately they give ground rapidly, fighting hard, retracking towards the gap between the farm and Woodnugget Wood. Quickly you order your reserve, a thousand men of Serakub, forwards into Hartwig Fell's

Farm, giving Gwyneth something to fall back on. If you infiltrated Honoric's camp last night and discovered the contents of three large wooden boxes, turn to **58**. If you do not know the contents of the boxes, turn to **68**.

49

You manage to tear yourself out of the dragon-vulture's clutches, but only by diving down towards the ground. Shadazar dives after you. She is right on your tail. Will you try to turn sharply (turn to **145**) or rise upwards sharply, inevitably slowing down as you do so (turn to **165**)?

50

The fleeing men's eyes fill with recognition and many pull up, shame on their faces. Soon you have rallied about eight hundred of them. You ride back to Colwyn's Mound with the cavalry, where their officers begin to organise them into a single unit. You can see Doré le Jeune fighting with the men of the Spires, defending the ditch bravely. Suddenly there are cries of alarm. From the Old Farm come two hundred monks of the Scarlet Mantis pounding up the hill to your position. 'They must have come from the Wickerwood!' cries Hengist, as he and his fellows crowd around you. The Corps of Bannermen surround you as the monks, in unnerving silence, fall upon your position. Already the cavalry is coming to your aid, but the monks seem intent on only one thing, getting to you and killing you.

Suddenly a man breaks through to face you. Your Orb glows brightly – magic sight reveals that it is an Old One, perhaps the same one you fought when you strove for the Crown of Irsmuncast what seems like ages ago. From its robes protrude tentacles, and its mouth is rimmed with long tentacular appendages. One writhing 'hand' is curled around a heavy glowing mace. Those battling groups of warriors nearby back away leaving a small arena.

'So, Avenger, you have come this far. But this is where your upstart reign ends,' it whispers sibilantly. You must fight it. You cannot kick or throw as you are on horseback, but you can use your mace-like Sceptre and your fists. Will you try a Tiger's Paw chop (turn to **60**), drive your Sceptre at it (turn to **70**) or spur your charger forwards and try to knock the Old One to the ground (turn to **80**)? If you use the Sceptre to attack it, you cannot use Inner Force to double the damage.

51

A crack, unnoticed over the years, runs around the raised square of marble. Pressing the square next to a slight discoloration causes it to revolve. There is the sound of shattering glass, and a spray of acid bathes your face. You fall back in agony as your flesh steams and smarts. The Seneschal comes to your aid but there is nothing he can do as you grit your teeth to stop yourself screaming. When the acid has finished doing its work, the skin of face is white and bubbled. Lose 3 Endurance. You are horribly disfigured. Note that your face is horribly scarred. The revolving marble has uncovered a hollow recess in which a broken phial of acid now lies. Turn to **111**.

52

You creep forwards stealthily. They have still not heard you when you stand centimetres behind one of the guards. You unleash a crippling Tiger's Paw chop at the guard's exposed neck and he goes down like a sack of potatoes. The other wheels around in astonishment, a cry of alarm on the tip of his tongue. You have only an instant in which to silence him, as you step forwards and execute a Leaping Tiger kick. His Defence is 7. If you hit him, turn to **102**. If you miss, turn to **112**.

53

You decide to use your Sceptre as a staff on your journey. You have realised that you can use its effect of enhancing your charisma by merely wishing it. The first leg of your journey takes you obliquely past the southern tip of the Rift, the Bowels of Orb, that great chasm like a rotting seam on the fruit that is Orb. In the caverns and catacombs that riddle its cliffs and descend to the centre of Orb dwells so much evil that the minds of men cannot even begin to comprehend. Somewhere far from the light of day lurk the cities of the Old Ones and others from the age before the coming of man. You decide to give the chasm a wide berth, but your eagle eyes notice a minute black speck circling far above you in the clear sky. It is joined by a mate, and you can guess from the patterns that they fly that they are carrion crows, as like as not sent to spy on you by Dark Elves from the Rift. You press on, anxious not to waste time. Turn to **243**.

54

Your army is in position. So is that of Honoric's. Everything is quiet – the lull before the storm. Suddenly a trumpet blast sounds from the serried ranks. A lone rider gallops out and shouts, 'Honoric, Lord of the Legion of the Sword of Doom, challenges Avenger, so-called Overlord of Irsmuncast, to an honourable duel on open ground between the opposing armies. Come forth and fight or forever be dishonoured.'

Doré le Jeune says: 'You must go, Overlord.' But Glaivas says: 'Don't be ridiculous, Avenger – a senseless risk.'

Will you accept Honoric's challenge (turn to **414**) or refuse it (turn to **64**)?

55

Of the city notables who had been so influential when you cast down the Usurper, four are either dead or flown. As you know, Parsifal, the head of the monastery of your god Kwon, was assassinated by Mandrake, the Guildmaster of Assassins from far away Wargrave Abbas. Since then he has been replaced by Hengist, a younger man who is a dangerous martial artist. Together you have already begun to retrain your fellow monks so that the martial arts tradition of the Temple to Kwon in Irsmuncast should be worthy of its name. The Lord High Steward, once the Usurper's instrument of subjugation, is dead, as you executed him yourself for his temerity when you took office. Foxglove, latterly the shrewd and captivating head of the Order of the Yellow Lotus, the secret informers, has disappeared without trace, though the rumour is that she betrayed Irsmuncast by revealing to the Dark Elves the weaknesses of the city's defences. Whatever the truth, her Order is no more. Golspiel and the other merchants are long departed from the city. You must look to trade if the city is to feed itself. The other notables, the rabble-rousing Demagogue, Gwyneth, Greystaff and Solstice, the High Priest of the inscrutable Templars to Time, have all survived. Turn to **31**.

56

You and Doré le Jeune ride as fast as you can to Colwyn's Mound and take up a position at the head of your troops. 'For Irsmuncast and freedom!' you shout, raising, the Sceptre high. Doré le Jeune shouts, 'For Rocheval!', and you both charge forwards. If you fought the duel with Honoric before the battle, turn to **76**. If you did not, turn to **86**.

57

The staircase leads directly down to the Throne Room. Partway down you see the Seneschal staggering aimlessly as if in pain. He has been one of many trusty henchmen during the difficult days of your overlordship and his face as he catches sight of you is an amusing mixture of surprise, joy and pity at the sight of your lost eye. 'Avenger,' he says, 'You have returned to be our salvation once again. I knew you would.' He is wounded and bleeding, but not near death. You motion towards the Throne Room. 'Is it safe?' The Seneschal nods, then there is the sound of uncouth orcish voices from below. Will you carry the Seneschal into the Throne Room (turn to **177**) or leap down the stairs to do battle (turn to **189**)?

58

You had told the White Mage of what you had seen some hours earlier. Standing nearby, he says quietly, 'My time has come, Overlord,' and then he mutters something inaudible. Suddenly he takes to the air, to the astonishment of all those on the Greenridge, and flies towards the Wickerwood. Just then three winged creatures, the Wyverns, flap up from behind Manor Ridge and streak towards the retreating forces of Irsmuncast. The White Mage, high in the sky, his robes glittering in the sun, flies to meet them with bolts of lightning, words of power and potent magic. The Wyverns encircle him, lungeing with their jaws and whipping their poison-barbed tails.

Antocidas and his mercenaries are fleeing the field completely, pursued by some of Honoric's cavalry. The larger part of the Bringers of Doom are preparing to charge Gwyneth and her retreating infantry. At the ford the pressure is increasing, and a courier reaches you asking that you order the cavalry of Aveneg to charge in an attempt to throw back the warriors of Mortavalon, who are trying to outflank your allies there. The men of Béatan from Serakub are now taking up a position in Hartwig Fell's Farm.

Will you order Gwyneth's cavalry to charge the flank of the Legion of the Sword of Doom, to try to make time for Gwyneth to pull back and order the cavalry of Aveneg to do as requested (turn to **78**) or order both units to charge the Legion in support of Gwyneth (turn to **88**)?

59

Dom snorts derisively. 'Then you know more than I do, Avenger. I have as yet been unable to unravel a strand of the future in which you are fated to rule Irsmuncast into the next year. I am unwilling to risk my city to save you. Fate has not vouchsafed me a full view of what shall come to pass. One of the other gods has persuaded her to hold the knowledge back from me, and so I can do nothing. I am sorry, Avenger. You have no idea how much it pains me to meet someone without hope, as indeed you must be,' With that he springs up from the rainbow throne and strides out of his Throne

Room. You are escorted from the Palace and asked to leave the city. Burning with indignation, you set off for Irsmuncast to look to the city's defences. Turn to **99**.

60

Your horse prances wildly as the Old One closes in and, leaning out of the saddle, you whip your hand down at its head.

OLD ONE
Defence against Tiger's Paw chop: 7
Endurance: 22
Damage: 1 Die + 2

If you have killed it, turn to **90**. If it still lives, it swings its mace at your ribs. Your Defence is 7. If it hits you, take damage in the normal way and then turn to **110**. If it misses you, will you use the Tiger's Paw chop again (return to the top of this, paragraph), spur your horse into it (turn to **80**) or hack at it with your Sceptre (turn to **70**)?

61

The scribes bring countless books and scrolls into Star Chamber and begin to pore over them. One of the first things you notice is that while the Manmarch looks more or less the same on all of the maps, they all disagree as to the precise geography and even the names of the cities outside the Manmarch. Will you ask for information about Upanishad (turn to **351**), Greydawn (turn to **381**), Serakub (turn to **391**), Wargrave Abbas (turn to **43**) or the Spires of Foreshadowing (turn to **401**)? If you are ready to make a decision as to which city you will seek as your ally, turn to **281**.

62

You turn on your heels and run into the night. You are closely followed, but you have soon lost your pursuers – few can track a ninja at night! Despondent, you return to the encampment of your army. Turn to **100**.

63

All eyes are turned aloft in awe as the battle for the sky begins. At the last moment before contact, you fling your wings out wide and crack them downwards, surging above Shadazar the dragon-vulture. Your claws rake her shoulders as she sails beneath you, and you turn more quickly than she can. The battle rages for some time, and now that you have discovered that you are more manoeuvrable you are gaining the advantage. The Trolls are attacking below, however, and you must finish this quickly. Will you try to drop on her from above like a swooping eagle (turn to **23**) or try to close your beak on her neck and snap it (turn to **47**)?

64

As you shout your refusal, a gasp of surprise goes up from your own forces. You cannot help but feel that your forces' morale has been affected. If your allies are the men of the Spires of Foreshadowing and of Fiendil, turn to **74**. If they are of Serakub and Aveneg turn to **84**.

65

Two of your flashing shuriken find their mark, spattering the remains of dead spider across the bare earth. One, however, still remains, and you have cast all your throwing stars. Will you climb the tree and use one of your sleeve irons to stave in the spider if it climbs the tree (turn to **143**) or pick up a nearby stone and hurl that (turn to **105**)?

66

The Old One lies at the feet of your charger. Looking up, you see that your charge has been wholly successful. The Legion is now in full retreat. Sensing a taste of victory, the rest of your army moves to the offensive. Soon the whole of Honoric's army is in full retreat with the Doomover Levies completely routed and fleeing pell-mell. Your forces are relatively well off. Some elements are too exhausted, such as the defenders at the farm, but you begin issuing orders for organising a pursuit with those still able to go on. Note that you are able to carry out a pursuit. Turn to **250**.

67

You look around the hundred Prodromese as you nervously try to decide what to say and in what manner to say it. The Sceptre at your side lends you confidence. The people seated in the tiered pews of the oval hall could hardly look more different one from another. Many proclaim the deity they serve through their dress. The followers of Béatan are unmistakable. They are spread evenly throughout the hall, but all wear the badge of the five-spoked Wheel of Myriad Possibility. Seated opposite you is a body of men and women who wear the sword and lozenge-shaped shield of Dama. On their right is a group of strange-looking men clad in greens and browns, each wearing a sprig of oak in their hair. You guess them to be the followers of Ilexkuneion, the god of animals and plants. Beyond them you are dismayed to note fifteen or so black whirlpool badges, and next to these a like number of purple and green spiders. Serakub has its share of evil-doers too. Fate and Torremalku the Slayer are also represented, and there are six young priestesses bearing the symbol of a crescent moon, but the identity of their god or goddess eludes you. They are a mixed audience indeed. There will be no secrecy here in the Boule. If you are hideously scarred, as a result of actions during your current adventure, turn to **285**. Otherwise, will you tell them of your father and ask them to honour his memory by granting troops for your campaign (turn to **77**), make much of the evil of the Legion of the Sword of Doom (turn to **127**) or invoke the power of the Sceptre as you describe the justice of your cause (turn to **147**)?

68

Three strange winged reptiles flap up from the area of Manor Ridge. To your horror you recognise Wyverns – enormously powerful beasts with poison-barbed tails. They streak towards the retreating women and begin to wreak terrible carnage. Gwyneth's cavalry charges to her aid but is met by a volley of crossbow bolts. The Bringers of Doom charge home, and before your very eyes your best troops are torn to shreds. Gwyneth goes down fighting, surrounded by a score or more of Honoric's Cataphracts. The battle is already lost. You can do nothing but order a general retreat. It is not long before this turns into a rout by the unrelenting pursuit of Honoric's forces. You are cut down trying to rally your troops, caught by a squadron of cavalrymen and killed almost in passing.

69

'Fate, who keeps the balance of all things, vouchsafes me glimpses of the future so that I may rule more wisely and to the greater glory of the goddess.'

'Then everything you do must turn to good?'

'Most things,' agrees Dom, 'save sometimes Fate herself will not show me the outcomes and then I must decide for myself.'

'And what of me?' you ask. 'What is my future?' Dom shakes his head solemnly. 'I have not yet unravelled a skein of the future which shows you as the ruler of Irsmuncast into the next year. The only possibility is if I ally with you against Doomover, but the vision of that future is closed to me. Another god has prevailed upon Fate to keep this hidden from me.'

Will you say that Honoric's ambitions will turn to the City of the Spires once he has Irsmuncast (turn to **79**) or implore him to help since he knows he is your only chance (turn to **89**)?

70

You hack down with your Sceptre. None of your Modifiers apply and you may not use Inner Force. If you hit the Old One, you will do 1 Die + 3 damage.

OLD ONE
Defence against Sceptre: 8
Endurance: 22
Damage: 1 Die + 2

If you have killed it, turn to **90**. If it still lives, it swings its mace at your ribs. Your Defence is 7. If it hits you, take damage in the normal way and then turn to **110**. If it misses you, will you use the Sceptre again (return to the top of this paragraph), spur your horse into it (turn to **80**) or use a Tiger's Paw chop (turn to **60**)?

71

It requires every ounce of your considerable strength to rip the emerald from its nesting-place in your face. Blood spurts, and you reel with pain. Part of the flesh of your cheek has been torn away in your sudden panic. Lose 3 Endurance. You are now hideously disfigured; note that your face is horribly scarred. There is the sound of uncouth orcish voices on the staircase below. You have overcome the pain and are ready to act. Will you leap down the staircase to give battle (turn to **233**) or, if you have the skill of Climbing, climb down the Palace tower to the smoke-obscured gardens below (turn to **247**).

72

You run past the second guard towards the camp. Several other guards arrive on the scene, but you skilfully manage to avoid them. However, word of your presence is spreading around the camp – you are alone amid an army of enemies. You try to avoid the hunters and you are successful until magicians and priests are brought in, using detective magic. Try as you might you are soon caught, overwhelmed and slain.

73

Fires rage everywhere. The bodies of your townsfolk litter the streets, and the gutters run with blood. Your people have not given up their city without a struggle, but everywhere you look, there are Orcs, Orcs sporting the emblem of a woman's head cut off at the neck, dripping blood. The Orcs of the Severed Head like nothing more than looting, despoiling and pillaging. You are close to despair, forced many times to hide in the shadows as groups of Orcs rush out of houses waving treasures, heirlooms of the families whose blood stains their maws blacker than night. At last you come to the windmill tower on Seven Post Road, an easy climb. Hanging beneath one of the windmill's great sails you survey the city.

The noise of chaos is all around: screaming, fighting, the sounds of Orcs and of men in pain. A bugle call rises stridently above the clash of arms and the cries of the wounded, bringing new hope. The great onion-shaped silhouette of the Temple to Time stands out blacker than the darkness, and for the first time you notice an orderly array of torches in the great sundial square before it. Casting off the hawser that checks the turning of the windmill, you cling to the sail as it carries you high above the highest roof, drop unseen on to a tiled gable and leap from rooftop to rooftop until you look down at the gathering in the square. What you see gladdens your heart. Turn to **33**.

74
If you decided to follow Doré le Jeune's advice and attack (using the map at **402**), turn to **104**. If you followed the advice of Gwyneth, to defend with left flank refused (using the map at **392**), turn to **94**. If you followed the counsel of Hickling, to hold out along the stream and river (using the map at **412**), turn to **114**.

75
All eyes are turned aloft in awe as hippogriff meets dragon-vulture head on. There is a great clash and feathers and scales float Orbwards. Shadazar's beak gouges into your bird-face and you try to peck out her eyes. Lose 3 Endurance. If you are still alive, you realise that the dragon-vulture is more powerful even than your hippogriff form. Locked together in combat, you begin to plummet to the ground. Will you try to break away (turn to **49**) or continue the battle (turn to **41**)?

76
A roar of approval thunders from the throats of your soldiers and you charge into battle. It is exhilarating as you plunge forwards riding hard and waving the Sceptre above your

head. The remaining crossbowmen still on the field of battle are just appearing around the rear of the Legion, but your hell-for-leather charge carries you into them before they have a chance to open fire. At the sight of you, Doré le Jeune and his Paladins, and the exulted ferocity of your warriors, they scatter and run. You drive on to slam into the rear of the Legion, cutting through it like a knife through butter. Doré le Jeune fights like a whirlwind, and the legionaries, caught unawares, begin to waver.

Suddenly, in the midst of the battle, a figure appears before you. Your Orb glows brightly – magic sight reveals that it is an Old One, perhaps the same one you fought when you strove for the Crown of Irsmuncast what seems like ages ago. From its robes protrude tentacles, and its mouth is rimmed with long tentacular appendages. One writhing 'hand' is curled around a heavy glowing mace. Those battling groups of warriors nearby back away, leaving a small arena.

'So, Avenger, you have come this far. But this is where your upstart reign ends,' it whispers sibilantly. You must fight it. You cannot kick or throw as you are on horseback, but you can use your mace-like Sceptre and your fists. Will you try a Tiger's Paw chop (turn to **168**), drive your Sceptre at it (turn to **178**) or spur your charger forwards and try to knock the Old One to the ground (turn to **188**)? If you use the Sceptre to attack it, you cannot use Inner Force to double the damage.

77

You tell them of your ancestry and of your struggle to restore the laws of Loremaster Szeged of Serakub, your father. You describe Irsmuncast and its people, saying how much they need military help, and then sit down at the end of your speech in an ominously silent hall.

The debate thereafter is stormy, but it becomes obvious before long that the vote will go against you. The followers of Dama are unwilling to go to war for the sake of your father's memory, and it was upon them you had counted for support. After the vote the head of the Boule, a learned fellow called Obuda Varhegyen, sympathises with you but explains that you will not find an ally in Serakub. You are forced to return to Irsmuncast to look to the defences of the city, but when Honoric invades his troops are too many and too powerful. You die defending the walls and Irsmuncast is taken.

78

Your orders are carried out. The assault on the ford is temporarily halted, but the Irsmuncast cavalry is intercepted by Honoric's Bringers of Doom and a cavalry skirmish ensues. Then, to your horror, Force-Lady Gwyneth herself is slain and her warriors, outnumbered five to one, begin to break up. Carnage ensues and they break and run.

The battle is already lost. You can do nothing but order a general retreat. It is not long before this turns into a rout by the unrelenting pursuit of Honoric's forces. You are cut down trying to rally your troops, caught by a squadron of cavalrymen and killed almost in passing.

79

Is your left eyeball an empty socket (turn to **119**), or do you see through the Orb of Kings (turn to **139**)?

80

You try to spur your horse forwards, but it rears back in horror from contact with the strange creature, enabling the Old One to dart in and swing its mace at you. Your Defence is 7. If it hits you, the attack will deal 1 Die + 2 damage and then you must turn to **110**. If it misses you, will you try a Tiger's Paw chop (turn to **60**) or hack at it with your Sceptre (turn to **70**)?

81

'Naught but a popinjay,' says Gwyneth as a tall thin man with a jerky step enters the Throne Room, kneels and touches his forehead to the floor. He wears the harlequin garb of a travelling entertainer and has a lute strapped across his back. His costume is pink and green, indicating that he has learned his skills on the Island of the Goddess at the school of Dithyrhambo. He is either a skilled minstrel or a charlatan. More important, though, is the fact that travelling players such as he see much of Orb and customarily tell the news of the world in the taverns of the cities that they visit. 'What is your name, student of Dithyrhambo?' you ask.

'Fidelio, Majesty,' he answers, and he begins to tell you his news. 'The Legion of the Sword of Doom is preparing for war, Majesty.' He pauses.

'What of it?' snaps Gwyneth.

'It is not easy to guess where the eye of Lord Honoric quests for glory, though I have heard rumours... I know not if they be true...' he trails off into silence.

'If not true, then of no use to me,' you say, not bothering to conceal your irritation.

'The vagabond wants money, Overlord' says Gwyneth, and she shows her contempt for this man by using the spitoon. Will you offer Fidelio gold (turn to **91**), command him to tell you all he knows (turn to **101**) or invite him to play at the royal table this evening (turn to **121**)?

82

The shuriken tears out the guard's throat and he collapses to the ground with a muted gurgle. The other guard turns in surprise and, unsure as to what has afflicted his comrade, kneels over him with his back to you. Instantly you leap forwards and deliver a crushing blow to the back of his neck, knocking him out. Hurriedly you don the armour and surcoat of one of the guards. You are now dressed as a swordsman of Vasch-Ro from the legion of the City of Aveneg. Turn to **122**.

83

Shadazar's lissom black form also changes shape before you. She sprouts green scaly wings and a cruelly barbed tail. Her head grows a hooked beak and her back is covered with grey feathers. She has become a dragon-vulture, larger and much more horrible than your hippogriff form. She launches herself into the air and soars towards you. You are at the same height. Will you meet her head on (turn to **75**) or try to gain height (turn to **63**)?

84

If you decided to follow Force-Lady Gwyneth's advice, to refuse the left flank (using the map at **14**), turn to **18**. If you followed the advice of Hivatala, to refuse the right flank (using the map at **34**), turn to **28**. If you followed the advice of Obuda Varhegyen, to form a defensive line along the stream (using the map at **24**), turn to **38**.

85

The speed and accuracy with which you cast your throwing stars is a dream to behold. The spiders' remains are smeared across the bare earth. You encircle them, watching the Dark Elf sorcerers, but each mounts his flying mount and they flap away into the growing dusk that seems to well up out of the Rift. Turn to **185**.

86

You lead the charge but even allowing for the Sceptre you feel that your presence has not really helped the men's morale. It seems they have lost confidence in you. The cavalry canters off the mound and charges forwards. But it suffers heavily from the rest of Honoric's crossbowmen, and although these give way before your cavalry the charge is largely ineffectual.

Finally the men of the Spires break and run, and the Legion of the Sword of Doom and the remaining cavalry pour through, wheeling around to roll up the rest of your army. Soon it is a full rout. You are caught in the open, trying to rally your forces, by a squadron of the Bringers of Doom and cut down almost in passing. But, perhaps, you will be remembered in a song.

87

The crossbow bolt speeding towards you is a blur of speed, but even before its shrieking whine has been perceived by the Orcs you have drawn up your legs out of the way and swept it from its path with a swipe of your iron-rodded sleeve. It buries itself in the back of an unfortunate Orc, but you have sprinted off into the haze of smoke and distanced yourself from pursuit in a twinkling. Turn to **73**.

88

Gwyneth's cavalry charges forwards, as does the cavalry of Aveneg, sweeping around the swordsmen of Irsmuncast's flank to get at the Legion of the Sword of Doom. Gwyneth's cavalry is intercepted by the Bringers of Doom and a cavalry skirmish ensues. But the Legion of the Sword of Doom is forced to turn and face the threat of a cavalry charge from the men of Aveneg, and Force-Lady Gwyneth is able to pull back to safety. Instantly your cavalry breaks off its attacks before it is cut off and retires to Crossway Copse. Gliftel's Elves unleash a volley of deadly arrows from Woodnugget Wood and the Legion of the Sword of Doom retires a few paces, where they and their cavalry regroup, preparing to assault Hartwig Fell's Farm. Turn to **98**.

89

'Pity is no motive to expose one's city to risk. I am sorry, Avenger. You cannot know how it pains me to see one without hope, as indeed you must now be.' With that he springs up from the throne and leaves his Throne Room. You are escorted from the Palace and asked to leave the city. Burning with indignation, you set off for Irsmuncast to look to the defences of the city. Turn to **99**.

90

The Old One, its head shattered, falls in a heap at your feet. If you ordered your cavalry and men of the Spires to charge the enemy at the beginning of the battle, or if Doré le Jeune disobeyed your orders and led them in a charge anyway, turn to **140**. If not – if your men did not charge – turn to **150**.

You tell Fidelio that you will pay a purseful of gold for his news, and he goes on: 'Some of the rumours have perhaps more substance to them than others. Honoric wishes for vengeance against you, Overlord, for what passed at Quench-heart Keep. Many on Orb know that you triumphed there over the Deathmage and Yaemon. Honoric has not forgotten the humiliation. He prepares to ride out to war against this fair city on the first day of Grimweird, a day that is sacred to Vasch-Ro, his God of War. You have until then to prepare for the onslaught.'

Gwyneth questions him as to the composition of Honoric's forces, but he knows no more than you can guess, that it will include the dreaded Legion of the Sword of Doom. He tells you some news from the City of the Spires, the long-standing enemy of Doomover. Some of the Tools of Fate are urging their king, Dom the Prescient, to wage war against Doomover if Honoric marches out, but he is reported to be concerned that the Forces of Death from the City of Mortavalon would join with Honoric if he did this. When Gwyneth has finished her searching questioning Fidelio takes his gold and leaves. You have him followed in case he departs the city immediately or acts suspiciously in any other way, but he goes to the Hostel from the Edge where he pays for a room for four nights. The rest of the day is spent in inspecting the city defences, and you tell Gwyneth before retiring that you will hold a council of war on the morrow. Gwyneth seems almost pleased as she bids you good night. Turn to **131**.

The shuriken whirs through the night air to strike the guard's armour-plated helm with a resounding clang. Both wheel towards you, their faces masks of surprise. Moments later they are shouting, 'Alarm, alarm!' and you can soon hear the sound of others running towards the commotion. Will you give up your attempt to spy out Honoric's camp (turn to **62**) or continue with your mission (turn to **72**)?

93

Unfortunately, the journey to Wargrave, through the Mountains of Vision, takes too long, and you realise too late that the passes through the mountains are impassable to armies at this time of year. You are forced to turn back and fight without an ally. The taste of defeat is bitter, but at least you die bravely on the field of battle.

94

See paragraph **392** for a map of the current positions. You can add notes to the map at **342** if necessary.

The sound of braying trumpets and shouted orders comes to you on the morning breeze. Honoric's soldiers on your far left begin to advance over Ruric's Bridge at a fast trot. When they have reached Bridgebeam, the Levies, the Legion of the Angel of Death and the Warrior Women of Horngroth begin to advance across the ford. Then a great guttural roar goes up from the Legion of the Sword of Doom and the massed cavalry. They surge forwards, charging hell for leather for the men of the Spires stationed between Hartwig Fell's Farm and Colwyn's Mound. You can see some of Honoric's officers cursing – it seems his cavalry are impetuous and have moved too early. In any case, the long line of cavalry led by the Bringer of Doom Cataphracts, whose horses are clad from head to toe in gleaming armour, plunge forwards, howling – a daunting sight. However, as they come nearer the ditch they begin to lose formation, some horses trip and all is confused for a moment.

Your Corps of Bannermen – some twenty standard-bearers with banners particular to individual units – stand nearby ready to signal your orders to your men. Doré le Jeune cries impetuously: 'Let me lead the cavalry to attack now, Overlord!' Will you signal for the cavalry of Irsmuncast and of the Spires to charge forwards, with the Paladin at their head, to attack the enemy as they try to cross the ditch (turn to **308**) or order your whole line to stand firm (turn to **318**)?

95

Grasping the Sceptre firmly, you thrust it aloft and declaim: 'I am the rightful Overlord of Irsmuncast nigh Edge. Acknowledge me as your ruler and I will pardon your crimes.' The Orcs appear unimpressed by your words. The chieftain gives the word to fire and your body is peppered by the Orcs' quarrels. Without you the city is doomed to evil and destruction.

96

If you infiltrated Honoric's camp last night and discovered the contents of three huge wooden boxes, turn to **176**. If you do not know the contents of the boxes, turn to **186**.

97

You are past the Dark Elves who guard the doorway before they even see you and you rush up the stairs towards the battlemented tower. The only enemies you meet on the way are Orcs who have discovered the Palace wine cellar. They are too drunk to hinder you. Soon you are at the top of the staircase.

Turn to **339**.

98

Then your attention is drawn to the ford, where the cavalry of Horngroth has charged the defenders. The men of Aveneg are taking heavy losses and are beginning to give ground slowly, fighting every centimetre of the way, but their position is looking more and more tenuous.

The threat of attack from the cavalry of the Legion of the Sword of Doom is such that Hengist urges you to move the command post to the knoll at Crossway Copse. Hurriedly you prepare to do so, but before you do will you order the cavalry of Serakub on the far left to race across the Old Bridge to the aid of Ba'al and his men at the ford (turn to **108**) or order the cavalry of Aveneg and Irsmuncast, now at Crossway Copse, to do so (turn to **118**)?

99

Without an ally your forces are hopelessly outnumbered by Honoric's troops. Irsmuncast is overrun and you die nobly defending its walls.

100

You find your army encamped near the village you passed when you first came up the valley. This is where the battle will be fought on the morrow. You go to your tent immediately to catch what sleep you can before dawn, when you will meet your commanders and advisors to decide a strategy. Turn to **342**.

101

Fidelio does not seem ruffled by your peremptory tone. He goes on: 'Some of the rumours have more substance than others. Honoric wishes for vengeance against you, Overlord. Many on Orb know what passed at Quench-heart Keep, that you triumphed over the Deathmage and Yaemon of the Order of the Scarlet Mantis. Honoric has not forgotten the humiliation. He prepares to ride out to war against this fair city on the first day of Grimweird, a day that is sacred to Vasch-Ro, his God of War. You have until then to prepare for the onslaught. ' With that he bows once more and backs towards the door. Gwyneth would stop him but you decide to let him go, giving in to Gwyneth when she suggests that an armed guard escort him to the city gates and forbid him to return on pain of death. You spend the rest of the day inspecting the city defences and tell Gwyneth that you will hold a council of war on the morrow. She seems almost pleased as she bids you good night. Turn to **131**.

102

Your kick is well judged. The ball of your foot takes him on the chin, snapping his head back and bowling him over, where he lies on the grassy earth, inert. Hurriedly you don the armour and surcoat of one of the guards. You are now dressed as a swordsman of Vasch-Ro, from the legion of the City of Aveneg. Turn to **122**.

The announcement of your imminent departure from Irsmuncast causes panic, but when you explain that you are going to find an ally who will help to protect the city, calm is restored. You declare a state of martial law and leave Force-Lady Gwyneth in charge, cautioning her to watch Lackland carefully but not to force any confrontation with the reverencers of Nemesis. To Lackland you say before you leave that you will fight for all the citizens and that the supporters of Nemesis will not suffer under your rule. After all, his forces outnumber Gwyneth's almost two to one. Antocidas is having a hard time stopping his mercenaries deserting, since there is precious little gold with which to pay them. In the interests of secrecy and quick movement you decide to travel to Greydawn alone. Have you read the words of Nebr'Volent of the Eyeless Face? If so, turn to **53**. If not, turn to **27**.

Refer to paragraph **402** for a map of the position. You may make any notes you wish on the map at paragraph **342** also.

Trumpets sound, banners wave and a shout goes up from the enemy. Honoric's massed cavalry, closely followed by the Legion of the Sword of Doom and the Legion of the Angel of Death, cross the stream at the ford, which causes them to lose formation and become disordered. They intend to reform on your side of the stream. Ahead of your cavalry, beyond the ditch, lies open ground and then the enemy, who wait unmoving. Doré le Jeune sits astride his horse at the head of the cavalry, looking back at you expectantly. Your Corps of Bannermen – twenty men each holding a banner particular to a certain unit – wait in readiness to issue your orders. An Elf stands at the edge of Woodnugget Wood, ready to convey signals to Gliftel.

Will you order Doré le Jeune to lead the cavalry, followed by the men of the Spires, in a charge at the Doomover line, with supporting flanking fire from the Elves in the wood (turn to **344**), order the men of Fiendil between Hartwig Fell's Farm and Woodnugget Wood to charge forwards and engage the Doomover cavalry while they are still re-forming (turn to **354**) or give the signal that no charge is to be made yet and that the Elves are to pour flanking fire on to any forces that attack the men of Fiendil between Hartwig Fell's Farm and Woodnugget Wood (turn to **364**)?

105

As you bend to pick up the stone, one of the Dark Elves speaks a spell of transmutation. The stone turns to runny treacle in your hand. You scrabble for another, but the same thing happens again. Too late you try to flee, but the executioner spider has jumped on to your leg. Small fangs break your skin and the poison courses through your veins. Death takes only seconds. Now Honoric and the forces from the Rift will carve up the fate of Irsmuncast.

106

Honoric's cavalry begins to founder and lose cohesion as it crosses the stream, but the men regroup and charge on, followed by the Levies, headed for your troops between the farm and Colwyn's Mound. The Legion of the Sword of Doom's crossbowmen, the Rain of Doom, unleash a deadly volley of bolts at the defenders between the farm and the Greenridge and draw back. The swordsmen of the Legion then charge forwards with a roar, assaulting your whole left flank with frightening ferocity. A bitter bloody mêlée ensues, and your men begin to falter and give ground. Only the men in the farm itself are holding their position. Honoric's cavalry, with a blood-curdling battle-cry, slams into the Warrior Women of Dama with a resounding crash, the ring of steel on steel. The Warrior Women hold firm, and the cavalry is flung back, but then the Levies, four thousand strong, follow up their charge. The women of Dama still seem to be holding well.

A messenger arrives to see you. It appears that the monks of the Scarlet Mantis are trying to force a passage through the Wickerwood, but the Elves are holding them back. A deadly cat and mouse game is being fought in the wood.

Will you order the men at the Old Farm and the cavalry

at Colwyn's Mound to swing around into the flank of the Levies (turn to **126**) or order Antocidas' mercenaries to hurry forwards and reinforce your hard-pressed left flank (turn to **116**)?

107

Only two of the Orcs react quickly enough to discharge their crossbows before you are sailing above their heads in a leap of supernatural proportions. If you have the skill of Arrow Cutting, turn to **87**. If not, one of the bolts strikes home, wounding you deeply. Lose 5 Endurance. If you survive then you stagger when you land, but you are still able to sprint into the haze of smoke and distance yourself from your pursuers. Turn to **73**.

108

As you hurriedly relocate to Crossway Copse, the cavalry of Serakub reaches the ford just in time to bolster up the flagging defenders. A brave, desperate charge and the attackers are hurled back across the ditch, only to come howling back again. As soon as the cavalry left Bridgebeam, the Doomover Levies charged across the bridge. The Warrior Women of Dama are cutting them down in droves, but whenever the Levies try to run they are met by the swords of the women of Horngroth and are forced to continue the assault. Your allies are holding fast, but they are slowly but surely taking casualties.

On the right, the Legion of the Sword of Doom rushes to the attack again with a blood-curdling scream. However, a light but deadly stream of arrows from Woodnugget Wood causes them to veer into the farm itself. Its wooden fences are much easier to defend, and the Legion is not making much headway, though the fighting is bitter and bloody. But the Bringers of Doom and the cavalry of Vasch-Ro come charging hell for leather around the edge of Hartwig Fell's Farm intent on swinging into the rear of Gwyneth's already badly mauled infantry.

Doré le Jeune says that the cavalry of Irsmuncast and Aveneg have no choice but to intercept them and asks you to lead the charge with him. Hengist quickly advises you not to go. 'You are too important to risk, Overlord,' he says. Will you order Doré le Jeune to lead the charge (turn to **138**) or lead the charge yourself (turn to **128**)?

109

No sooner do you concentrate on the form of a hippogriff than you become one. It was a polymorph potion, and you have changed your form. Now you tower above your fellows, a great eagle-headed horse with enormous wings. The Sceptre falls into a flowerbed as your costume changes. You flex your feathered wings and as a magical beast, the beast of your house, you soar up towards Shadazar as she holds her hands aloft. As you approach she speaks a few words in a language you don't understand and throws off her purple robe. Turn to **83**.

110

As the blow connects, you feel a surge of sorcerous energy that emanates from the black glowing mace threatening to engulf you. Make a Fate Roll, but apply −2 to your Fate Modifier for this roll only. If Fate smiles on you, turn to **120**. If Fate turns her back on you, turn to **130**.

111

Inside the recess, beyond the remains of the broken acid phial, lies a leather pouch. Inside the pouch you find a tattered piece of parchment. Across its top in bold red letters of an ornate cursive script are the words 'The Sceptre of Ruling Among Friends'. Below these words is the hippogriff emblem and then more writing: 'The rightful wielder of the Sceptre of Ruling Among Friends shall be received as a beneficent leader by all those who are not the wielder's enemies. They shall be disposed to follow the wielder unto the ends of Orb or even as far as the Valley of Death if his cause be just and righteous according to the noble precepts of the Gods of Law. He need only grasp the Sceptre and wish to use its power.' The parchment bears a signature: 'Nebr'Volent of the Eyeless Face.' Perhaps this Nebr'Volent was a court magician who fashioned the Sceptre as an aid to the Overlords of the city. Your reverie is disturbed suddenly. The uncouth orcish voices and the hammering on the doors stop abruptly. There is silence, then an almighty boom as if a battering ram is being brought to bear on the doors of the Throne Room. The doors burst asunder and a great grey-skinned Cave Troll, three metres tall and almost as large as the great doorway, lumbers into the room. It stumps ponderously to the attack. Will you use the Leaping Tiger kick (turn to **347**), the Iron Fist punch (turn to **337**) or the Whirlpool throw (turn to **327**), or, if you were taught Kwon's Flail in a previous adventure, will you use the opportunity to open with this kick (turn to **357**)?

112

At the last moment the guard manages to twist aside; your foot grazes his cheek. Instantly he shouts, 'Alarm, alarm! A ninja! Alarm!' Moments later many men are rushing towards this spot. Will you give up your attempt to spy out Honoric's camp (turn to **62**) or try to continue with your mission (turn to **72**)?

113

The dragon-vulture returns to the battlemented tower above the Palace and turns back into Shadazar. Pausing only to wrap her cloak around her, she begins the Incantation of Heavenly Wrath once more. The Trolls are now attacking your troops. Will you attack them (turn to **363**) or try to slip past them and sneak back into the Palace (turn to **371**)?

114

See paragraph **412** for the map of current positions. You may make any notes you wish on the map at paragraph **342** also. Trumpets sound, banners wave and a great cry goes up from the enemy. The troops at the ford charge forwards to engage the men of Fiendil there but not the Legion of Death, which hangs back. As the troops cross the ditch they lose formation somewhat, taking the impetus out of their charge. It looks as if the men of Fiendil are standing firm. The Levies on the far left do nothing; the women of Dama glare across the bridge at them, shaking their fists. But it is on the right that the fighting is fiercest. The two thousand crossbowmen, the Rain of Doom, run forwards with military precision and open fire at the men nearest Woodnugget Wood, causing many casualties. Some of the priestesses of Avatar are busy there already. The Legion, all five thousand, advances close behind. An Elf emerges from the wood and signals to you – he is asking for orders. Your Corps of Bannermen, twenty warriors with banners particular to your units, are ready to signal to units anywhere on the battlefield. You order Gliftel to open fire on the Legion of the Sword of Doom when it launches an attack. Turn to **134**.

115

You manage to crush the spider with the sleeve iron and you jump down from the tree and spin around, looking from one of the Dark Elves to another. To your joy and surprise, they remount their giant crows, which flap away into the dusk that seems to pour out of the Rift like a fog. Turn to **185**.

116

You ride forwards and order Antocidas to reinforce the left flank, but he just looks at you evenly and says: 'Yes, Overlord, if you pay us an extra talent on return to Irsmuncast.' You gasp in outrage and anger. A talent is the weight of a man in pure gold, the currency with which a city is run. Will you refuse and curse him for a money-grabbing swine (turn to **136**) or swallow your anger and agree (turn to **146**)?

117

No sooner do you fix your concentration on the form of a roaring bull than you become one. It was a polymorph potion, and you have actually changed your form into that of a bull with fearsome horns and a thick muscular neck. Your gear and costume have changed too. Roaring mightily, you charge towards the Palace gates as five great Cave Trolls lumber out to do battle. Your first charge knocks one of the three-metre-tall Trolls to the ground and you gore it badly. Then there is a great crack in the sky and a bolt of blue lightning strikes the ground right next to you. Shadazar has called down a bolt from the heavens. It has not killed her Trolls, but several mercenaries and shieldmaidens lie dead. Your thick hide has been badly scorched. Only your bull's form has saved you from being turned into a charred husk, but you have lost 5 Endurance. If you are still alive, the shock has caused you to revert to your normal form. Taking advantage of the confusion, you recover the Sceptre that had fallen onto a flowerbed and try to slip into the Palace once more. Turn to **97**.

118

As you hurriedly move to Crossway Copse, your cavalry reinforces the ford just in time. But then the Legion of the Sword of Doom is unleashed on the farm. The Bringers of Doom, now amassed again, come charging hell for leather around the side of Hartwig Fell's Farm straight at Crossway Copse. There are no troops available for you to call on. Long before the cavalry of Serakub can come to your aid, you, Doré le Jeune and Glaivas have been overwhelmed and slain. Perhaps you will be remembered in a song.

119

'Your skein of destiny has been unhooked from the loom, Avenger. The day of your death draws nigh. I cannot help you. Pity is no motive to expose one's city to risk. I am sorry, Avenger. You cannot know how it pains me to see one without hope, as indeed you must now be.' With that he springs up from the throne and leaves his Throne Room. You are escorted from the Palace and asked to leave the city. Burning with indignation, you set off for Irsmuncast to look to the defences of the city. Turn to **99**.

Turn to **99**.

120

You manage to overthrow whatever magical force threatened you. The Old One growls in frustration. Will you try a Tiger's Paw chop (turn to **60**), hack at it with your Sceptre (turn to **70**) or spur your horse forwards into the Old One (turn to **80**)?

121

Dinner that evening is a quiet affair, just yourself and twenty or so sycophantic courtiers. Indeed, there are more servants than guests, but you go through with this rigmarole for the sake of morale. Fidelio senses the prevailing mood and he sings the ballad of the Honest Tinker, a fable about how a good man triumphs over adversity in the end because he leads his life according to the moral code he believes in. Then he plays something more stirring and you are soon marvelling at the skill of the bards of the Island of the Goddess. Looking around, you see that he is well on the way to captivating the hearts of most of the ladies present.

Next he sings the song of the Orb of Kings. The Orb is a green gem that one of the erstwhile kings of Serakub placed in his eye so that he could see invisible beings, but in the end he was killed in his sleep for the gem by ruffians who did not know who it was they killed. At the end of the song he dedicates it to you.

When he finishes his minstrelsy there is rapturous applause and you beckon him to join you at your table. He tells you all of the news that may be of use to you, or so it seems. 'Honoric desires vengeance, Overlord. Many on Orb know what came to pass at Quench-heart Keep, when you triumphed over the Deathmage and Yaemon, leader of the Order of the Scarlet Mantis. Honoric has not forgotten the humiliation. He is preparing to ride out to war on the first day of Grimweird, a day that is sacred to Vasch-Ro, his God of War. You have until then to prepare for the onslaught.'

Fidelio also tells you that there is much debate at the court of Dom the Prescient, the king of the ancient enemy of Doomover, the City of the Spires of Foreshadowing. Some of the Tools of Fate, the chosen heroes of that goddess, wish to go to war against Honoric if he marches out, but Dom fears that the Forces of Death from Mortavalon will join Honoric if they go to war. You thank Fidelio for his help and send word that you will call a council of war in the morning.

When you retire to the royal bedchamber, the words of Fidelio's ballad of the Orb of Kings are running around and around your head. Do you already have the power to see invisible beings? If so, turn to **157**. If not, turn to **141**.

122

Unnoticed, you thread your way through the camp fires, among soldiers of many cities who are laughing and joking for the most part – it seems confidence is high. Then you come to a camp fire where a loud argument is raging between a woman warrior, whom you recognise as a follower of the goddess Fell-Kyrinla, the Man-Hater, from the City of Horngroth, and one of the men of the Legion of the Sword of Doom, from Doomover. An officer comes over to intercede before the two antagonists come to blows. You can see there is no love lost between these allies. Turn to **132**.

123

The emerald Orb seems to glow threateningly as you raise it to your empty eye socket. It slides neatly into place and the flesh around it begins to creep so that the Orb is being sucked into place within your head. Will you tear the Orb out before it is too late (turn to **71**) or leave the emerald to embed itself (turn to **353**)?

Gwyneth stands and says, 'First let us hear the reports of our scouts,' and she indicates Glaivas. Glaivas says, 'This is what we can determine of Honoric's forces,' and reads out a report. He then hands it to you.

THE ARMY OF HONORIC

Legion of the Sword of Doom	5,000 swordsmen
	2,000 crossbowmen, the Rain of Doom
	500 cavalry (Cataphracts), the Bringers of Doom
Legion of Aveneg	1,000 swordsmen
Legion of the Spires	1,000 swordsmen
Women of Horngroth	1,000 swordswomen
	500 cavalry
Men of Mortavalon	1,000 spearmen of Moraine
	1,500 Swordsmen of Death, the Legion of the Angel of Death
	500 Lancers of Death, the Wings of Death
Monks of the Scarlet Mantis	200
Doomover Levies	4,000
	———
A total of some	18,200 troops

'We can field about 10,000 men, heavily outnumbered. And the Legion of the Sword of Doom are reckoned to be the best troops in all the Manmarch,' adds Glaivas. Turn to **382**.

125

No sooner do you fix your concentration on the form of a snail than you become one. It was a polymorph potion, and you have actually changed your form into that of a two-centimetre-high snail. The Sceptre that you were holding falls on you...

126

Your orders are carried out to good effect and the Levies are forced to withdraw with heavy losses. But by this time the Legion of the Sword of Doom has stormed the farm and your left flank is in full rout. Honoric's cavalry regroups, and soon your whole army has been rolled up from the left and routed. You are caught in the open, trying to rally your forces, by a squadron of the Bringers of Doom and slain out of hand.

127

As soon as you mention Honoric and the Legion of the Sword of Doom there is a stirring among the worshippers of Dama and you remember how the sage Vertégal describes the battle between Dama, Shieldmaiden of the Gods, and Vasch-Ro, god of mortal combat, He who sows for the Reaper, in the Book of the Gods. Warming to your task, you expand upon this to say that you feel you have been born with a mission. Will you say that your mission is to check the spread of the followers of Vasch-Ro in the Manmarch (turn to **167**) or that you feel you were born to make sure that the followers of Nemesis within your city do not subjugate the people again (turn to **207**)?

128

You gallop forwards on your white charger, Doré le Jeune and his Paladins beside you, to take up a position at the head of your cavalry. 'For Irsmuncast and freedom!' you cry, lifting your Sceptre high, as Doré le Jeune shouts, 'For Rocheval!' If you fought the duel with Honoric before the battle, turn to **158**. If you refused to fight, turn to **148**.

129

Using your skill of ShinRen you can tell that Peisistratus and Herris Alchmeonid are not to be trusted. Certainly you judge that when they find out that the lands you have offered border the Rift they will not be useful allies. Ogg Red-hand the Wolfen is far too dangerous to trust. Accordingly you decide to try to make Serakub your ally instead, but you will have to run all the way to arrive in time. Turn to **235**.

You feel a cold numbing your very soul – some part of you has been sucked into the mace. If you have no points of Inner Force left, turn to **334**. Otherwise, lose 1 point of Inner Force. Will you try a Tiger's Paw chop (turn to **60**) hack at the Old One with your Sceptre (turn to **70**) or spur your horse forwards in an attempt to knock the Old One over (turn to **80**)?

The war council consists of Antocidas the One-Eyed, leader of the mercenaries who helped you to defeat Shadazar, and the heads of the various powerful temples of Irsmuncast: Solstice from the Temple to Time, Hengist from the Temple to Kwon, Gwyneth from the Temple to Dama, Greystaff from the Temple to Avatar, and a man whom you have not yet met, Lackland, the Lord High Steward's successor in the Temple to Nemesis and head of that part of the Usurper's army that is still in existence. Gwyneth begins by summarising the threat posed by Honoric and reviewing the troops with which you must try once more to save the city.

Gwyneth herself commands eighteen hundred sword-arms under the banner of Dama, Shieldmaiden of the Gods, eight hundred of whom are well-armoured cavalry. High Priest Lackland, or, as he insists on styling himself at the war council, General Lackland, commands three and a half thousand men and Orcs, the remnants of the Usurper's army, who were not conspicuously loyal when Shadazar overran the city, although they did not actually join the forces from the Rift. They are all footsoldiers, and less effective than Gwyneth's soldiers, who are élite battle-hardened troops. In addition to these, the Demagogue commands the affections of the hastily assembled peasant militia, numbering perhaps ten thousand but lacking discipline and weapons, and unlikely to stand up well to the rigours of a campaign. If you have played Book 4: *OVERLORD!* and were protected by a samurai bodyguard under Onikaba, turn to **201**. Otherwise turn to **221**.

You find yourself standing near a group of men discussing the strength of their allies. These men are from Honoric's own troops, the Legion of the Sword of Doom, from Doomover. They regard themselves as élite warriors, the best in the Manmarch – and you know this is probably true. They regard the women of Horngroth as sound fighters but untrustworthy. Their discussion goes on to the men of the legions of Aveneg and the Spires: regular troops, but not as good as themselves. The group then derides the Doomover Levies, four thousand men, well armed but of poor quality. They seem to have particularly strong contempt for these, the militia of their city.

You are mulling over the implication of what you have overheard when a loud voice sounds in your ear. An officer of the Doomover legion is addressing you. 'What are you, an Aveneg legionary, doing here among the camp fires of the Legion of the Sword of Doom?' he cries harshly. 'You know it is out of bounds for the likes of you!' Some of the nearby soldiers look around with curious faces. You will have to talk your way out of this one. What will you say:

'I am sorry, sir. I seem to have lost my way. I was looking for the camp quartermaster. We need more salt beef rations.' Turn to **142**.

'I have messages from the captain-general of the Aveneg legion for Lord Honoric, sir.' Turn to **152**.

'I am looking for a priest of Vasch-Ro to preside over a religious ceremony for my troop of the Aveneg legion.' Turn to **162**.

The announcement of your imminent departure from Irsmuncast causes panic, but when you explain that you are going to find an ally who will help to protect the city, calm is restored. You declare a state of martial law and leave Force-Lady Gwyneth in charge, cautioning her to watch Lackland carefully but not to force any confrontation with the reverencers of Nemesis. To Lackland you say before you leave that you will fight for all the citizens and that the supporters of Nemesis will not suffer under your rule. After all, his forces outnumber Gwyneth's almost two to one. Antocidas is having a hard time stopping his mercenaries deserting, since there is precious little gold with which to pay them. In the interests of secrecy and quick movement you decide to travel to the Spires alone. Have you read the words of Nebr'Volent of the Eyeless Face? If so, turn to **163**. If not, turn to **219**.

Suddenly the crossbowmen pull back in good order. There is a great rippling shout and the Legion charges forwards with drill-like precision. The massed cavalry also breaks into a full-blooded charge with whooping cries and howls. The Elves pour a deadly rain of arrows into the flank of the Legion, whose ranks begin to lose cohesion. As the whole charge passes across the ditch, the Legion becomes further disordered. It is only because of this that your whole flank is not swept away instantly when the charge crashes into the defenders with terrible force. The priests and mages on each side are hurling spells at each other – a number of swords of the Legion have sorcerous powers like the sword of Honoric – and your Orb picks up waves of fear-spells washing over your lines. Your men are wavering, save those nearest the wood, where the arrows of the Elves are proving decisive. If you know of the contents of three large boxes in Honoric's camp and have informed the White Mage of them, turn to **144**. If not, turn to **154**.

135

There is nothing more you can gain by studying the Orb and Sceptre. There is a noise of uncouth orcish voices on the staircase below. Will you leap down to do battle (turn to **233**) or, if you have the skill of Climbing, climb down the outside of the Palace tower to the smoke-obscured gardens below (turn to **247**)?

136

He smiles and begins to march his men off the field of battle. The Legion of the Sword of Doom has stormed the farm and your left flank is in full rout. Honoric's cavalry regroups, and soon your whole army has been rolled up from the left and routed. You are caught in the open, trying to rally your forces, by a squadron of the Bringers of Doom and slain out of hand.

137

You spin round without warning and tense yourself. There is a terrible pain in the back of your head as something starts to crush your skull. Whatever it was that attacked the Seneschal had not been trying to get behind you after all. Your skull feels as if it is caught in giant nutcrackers. Lose 3 Endurance as the blood pounds deafeningly in your ears. If you are still alive, you manage to twist agilely and turn to get a look at your assailant. Turn to **149**.

138

Doré le Jeune and his Paladins gallop away, and almost without pausing lead your cavalry in a breakneck charge. As the two sides close, the Bringers of Doom raise their swords high. For the first time you notice that many of them have black glowing blades. It becomes clear that they have a similar effect to Honoric's sword Sorcerak, for fear radiates from them like a wave of nauseous horror. The two sides come together with a resounding crash, the clash of steel on steel. The cavalry of Aveneg is met by the Bringers of Doom and many of your men are killed instantly by the impact of the heavily armoured horses and their riders. But it is the wave of fear that finally ends it. The men of Aveneg break and run. Gwyneth's cavalry fights on grimly, but the Bringers of Doom charge on, virtually unchecked, to slam into the rear of Gwyneth's infantry. Attacked from both sides, they fall apart and are annihilated in seconds. Force-Lady Gwyneth falls under a hail of blows. The battle is lost as the Legion of the Sword of Doom begins to roll up your whole flank. Your army is soon routed, and you are caught in the open, trying to rally your soldiers, and slain by a squad of the cavalry of Horngroth.

139

'Very well, Avenger. Though I risk plunging my people into war against my two most powerful neighbours I will be your ally. I will give you four of my most puissant Tools of Fate, Happening the Mage, Kelmic the Warrior, Toller, his twin, and Hoitekh the Priest. They will lead the Cavalry of the Wheel, five hundred heavy horses, and three thousand footsoldiers, among the best in the Manmarch. In addition I will ask Whimsical the Theocrat to send troops from Fiendil to your aid. He is in my debt. I am sure he will not refuse me this. His contribution will not fall far short of my own if I know Whimsical. He hates to be outdone.' When you set out on your return journey to Irsmuncast your step is light and your heart buoyed up with hope. Turn to **369**.

Hengist and his comrades surround you, fending off the attacks of the monks with kicks and throws. They are the best martial artists the Temple of Irsmuncast has to offer. At last the cavalry arrives on the scene and the monks, outnumbered, are forced to fall back with heavy losses. On the left flank the Legion of Doomover and the Legion of the Angel of Death are still struggling to take the farm. All your troops are engaged there now, and a vicious stand-up fight is going on, men trading blows and dying where they stand. The men of the Spires are still holding the stream, but are being forced back slowly.

If you infiltrated Honoric's camp last night and found out the contents of three large wooden boxes, turn to **270**. If you do not know what the boxes contain, turn to **260**.

It is strange, you muse, that you, Avenger, who has but one good eye in your head should be the possessor of a green Orb such as that in the ballad. You take it out and gaze at it. It is roughly the right size to fit into your empty eye socket. Will you put it in place to see if anything happens (turn to **151**) or stow it safely until you can find out more about it (turn to **131**)?

'Well, you're way off course, soldier,' he says. The quartermaster's stores are near Lord Honoric's tent, over there.' And he points away to the left. Thanking him, you press on in the indicated direction. You come to a large open area at the centre of which rests a massive red pavilion adorned with sword symbols of Vasch-Ro, obviously the tent of Honoric for it is also surrounded by guards. A curiously indeterminate figure in grey robes approaches the pavilion. As he is about to enter, you feel a strange itching in your eye socket where the green Orb seems to pulsate under the eye-patch. Quickly you lift the patch. The vision revealed is of something strange and inhuman entering the pavilion, but there is not enough time to determine exactly what. You are taking a terrible risk just standing near Honoric's pavilion, so you move on. Turn to **172**.

143

Quickly you scramble up the tree and, tearing the cloth of your ninja costume, slip out one of the iron rods that you use as sleeve irons. The spider scurries up the dead bark of the tree at undiminished speed, and at the last moment leaps upwards at your outstretched hand. Make an Attack Roll against a Defence of 7. None of your Modifiers apply. If you succeed, turn to **115**. If you do not, turn to **175**.

144

The White Mage, standing nearby, says, 'My time has come.' He mutters something inaudible and then takes to the air, to the astonishment of all those on the Greenridge. He flies on towards the Wickerwood. Then, to your horror, you see the monks of the Scarlet Mantis pour out of the Wickerwood and into the flank of the men nearest the wood. Their assault is devastating, and combined with the Wings of Death and the cavalry of Horngroth, a large block about five hundred strong begin to give ground desperately only moments away from a full rout. If they break, it is likely that the rest will follow under the awful pressure of the full might of the Legion. Even now, all two thousand of the crossbowmen are moving to Woodnugget Wood to flush out Gliftel's Elves.

Will you order the cavalry of the Spires and Glaivas' Rangers to close in an attempt to shore up the fast-growing gap and then order up your reserves (turn to **164**) or order the whole line to fall back on Hartwig Fell's Farm (turn to **174**)?

145

You turn as sharply as you can, but Shadazar stretches out her long dragon-vulture head and catches your hind leg. Soon you are embroiled in vicious combat again and falling to Orb.

Turn to **41**.

146

He turns away and bellows orders and his men move off at a run to reinforce the left flank. They arrive just in time to stem the tide. The bitter struggle goes on. Honoric's cavalry has charged once again, and the Warrior Women on the right flank are beginning to give ground. Then to your left you see, galloping towards you, Glaivas, with perhaps ten of his Rangers left. He has held the bridge for as long as possible, but now three thousand warriors are filing across. You will have to act quickly. Will you order the cavalry of Irsmuncast, the Dama cavalry of Serakub and the four hundred men at the Old Farm to charge the Doomover Levies and their cavalrymen (turn to **156**) or ride forwards and personally lead them in a charge against the Levies (turn to **166**)?

147

Soon after you begin your speech, which is an honest one summarising the difficult position you find yourself in as Overlord of Irsmuncast and your hopes and aspirations, you invoke the friendly power of the Sceptre. Your charisma is subtly increased and your voice carries a compelling ring of truth and understanding. Looking around, you can see that your actions have polarised the feeling of the Boule. The followers of Nemesis and Nullaq, the Spider Queen, scowl at you with ill-concealed distaste. Others seem receptive to your words, but it may be that some of the Prodromese have detected your use of magic. At length your speech is done and you sit down to loud applause and some hissing. Turn to **217**.

There is silence behind you, and the cavalry charges forward. As the two sides close, the Bringers of Doom raise their swords high. For the first time you notice that many of them have black glowing blades. It becomes clear that they have a similar effect to Honoric's sword Sorcerak, for fear radiates from them like a wave of nauseous horror. The two sides come together with a resounding crash, the clash of steel on steel. The cavalry of Aveneg is met by the Bringers of Doom and many of your men are killed instantly by the impact of the heavily armoured horses and their riders. But it is the wave of fear that finally ends it. The men of Aveneg break and run. Gwyneth's cavalry fights on grimly, but the Bringers of Doom charge on, virtually unchecked, to slam into the rear of Gwyneth's infantry. Attacked from both sides, they fall apart and are annihilated in seconds. Force-Lady Gwyneth falls under a hail of blows. The battle is lost as the Legion of the Sword of Doom begins to roll up your whole flank. Your army is soon routed, and you are caught in the open, trying to rally your soldiers, and slain by a squad of the cavalry of Horngroth.

149

All you can see is a red glow before you. You take several steps back until you are stopped by a clammy wall behind you. Turn to **181**.

150

If the Wyverns routed your cavalry (and then you were able to rally them), turn to **170**. If the White Mage dealt with the Wyverns before they could attack your troops, turn to **160**.

151

The emerald Orb seems to glow threateningly as you raise it to your empty eye socket. It slides neatly into place and the flesh around it begins to creep so that the Orb is being sucked into place within your head. Will you tear the Orb out before it is too late (turn to **161**) or leave the emerald to embed itself (turn to **171**)?

The officer narrows his eyes suspiciously. 'Indeed – where then is the insignia of the Corps of Couriers? You are not dressed as a messenger. Show me these messages – or are you a spy?' The officer signals to his men and some of them rise up and approach you. Will you try to make a run for it (turn to **202**) or attack the officer (turn to **212**)?

You visit Solstice, who promises to change the passage of time so that you can arrive at Upanishad within a tenday and lead a fleet to attack Doomover by sea, but the spell that he puts you under makes everything happen impossibly fast for you to grasp. Your mind and your body are no longer as one, and your powers of leadership and quickness in battle are lost. So too is the city, for without allies you cannot withstand the Legion of the Sword of Doom.

Then, to your horror, you see the monks of the Scarlet Mantis pour out of the Wickerwood and into the flank of the men nearest the wood. Their assault is devastating, and combined with the Wings of Death and the cavalry of Horngroth, a large block about five hundred strong begin to give ground desperately only moments away from a full rout. If they break, it is likely that the rest will follow under the awful pressure of the full might of the Legion. Even now, all two thousand of the crossbowmen are moving to Woodnugget Wood to flush out Gliftel's Elves. You order the cavalry of the Spires and Glaivas' Rangers to close in an attempt to shore up the fast-growing gap, and then order up your reserves. Turn to **244**.

The Cave Troll waves its club menacingly as you step within range. It strikes, but you spin aside and grapple its thick waist. The Troll's momentum carries it forwards and you succeed in toppling it over, but it twists and powerfully changes the angle of its fall so that you are pinioned beneath its bulk. It gouges the club's spikes into your back, and, just as you are squirming free, two of the spectating Orcs scurry forwards and bury their swords in you, killing you instantly.

156

The cavalry charges forwards, but it becomes bogged down in a skirmish with the enemy and your right flank is not relieved before time runs out. The three thousand swordsmen that had just crossed the bridge rapidly scale the Greenridge and envelop the flank of the warriors of Béatan from Serakub. Inevitably, your whole flank gives way and the farm is stormed. Soon your whole army is in full retreat. You are caught in the open, trying to rally your forces, by a squadron of the Bringers of Doom and slain out of hand.

157

It is clear that Fidelio matched his words to his audience, for he could not miss the polished emerald eye that swivels in your head in time with your natural one. Was his dedication a warning or a threat? You rest that night with caution, but no ruffians disturb your sleep and you walk into the war council in the morning to address the peril facing Irsmuncast. Turn to **131**.

158

A roar of approval thunders from the throats of your soldiers and you charge into battle, 1,200 warriors at your back. It is exhilarating as you plunge forwards, riding hard and waving the Sceptre above your head.

As the enemy rides to meet you, the Bringers of Doom hold their swords up. You notice that many of them have black glowing blades. It becomes clear that they have a similar effect to Honoric's sword Sorcerak, for fear radiates from them like a wave of nauseous horror. But using the power of the Sceptre to inspire loyalty, you sense that this is counteracting the effects of the fear-magic. The two sides meet with a resounding crash and the ring of steel on steel. You find yourself face to face with a cavalryman of the Bringers of Doom, a Cataphract, clad from head to toe in

fishscale armour, but you manage to despatch him. The rolling mêlée careers around, a desperate and vicious fight with no quarter given or asked.

Suddenly, in the midst of the battle a figure appears before you, strangely on foot. Your Orb glows brightly – magic sight reveals that it is an Old One, perhaps the same one you fought when you strove for the Crown of Irsmuncast what seems like ages ago. From its robes protrude tentacles, and its mouth is rimmed with long tentacular appendages. One writhing 'hand' is curled around a heavy glowing mace. Those battling groups of warriors nearby back away, leaving a small arena.

'So, Avenger, you have come this far. But this is where your upstart reign ends.' it whispers sibilantly. You must fight it. You cannot kick or throw as you are on horseback, but you can use your mace-like Sceptre and your fists. Will you try a Tiger's Paw chop (turn to **168**), drive your Sceptre at it (turn to **178**) or spur your charger forwards and try to knock the Old One to the ground (turn to **188**)? If you use the Sceptre to attack it, you cannot use Inner Force to double the damage.

159

On the next day you are roused from your bed with unlooked-for good tidings. Your old friend Glaivas awaits you in the Throne Room with twenty Rangers who have come to champion your cause. You rejoice, knowing that if each has the wisdom and skill of Glaivas they are worth many times their number in battle. Glaivas proves invaluable in helping you to plan your strategy. He also brings news of troops marching south of the city from the Rift, either to attack the city or to join up with Honoric's forces, something you must prevent at all costs.

Later that day you feel as if you have been plunged into a tale of olden times, as a company of two hundred Wood Elves joins your ranks from the woods west of Sundial. They are few in number but each carries a stout yew bow, and Gwyneth tells you that each one is probably a better marksman than anyone in the Manmarch cities.

You have had much time to rest. If you are wounded, restore your Endurance to 20. Turn to **169**.

160

Hengist and his comrades surround you, fending off the attacks of the monks with kicks and throws. They are the best martial artists the Temple of Irsmuncast has to offer. At last the cavalry arrives on the scene and the monks, outnumbered, are forced to fall back with heavy losses.

On the left flank, the Legion of Doomover and the Legion of the Angel of Death are still struggling to take the farm. All your troops are engaged there now, and a vicious stand-up fight is going on, men trading blows and dying where they stand. To your horror you see a line of horsemen, with the heavy Cataphracts of the Bringers of Doom shod from head to toe in glowing scaled armour at the centre, thundering towards you from the direction of Tallhill. They have circled around your left flank, driving straight for the back of your warriors at the stream, aiming to crush your men as if between hammer and anvil, the hammer the cavalry and the anvil the Doomover Levies and Honoric's allies. Already the 'anvil' has crossed the ditch and is forcing your men back. They could break at any time. You must act now.

There are about 2,000 enemy cavalry, and you fielded about 1,700. Will you order all your cavalry to charge back and meet the enemy cavalry head on (turn to **240**) or take the majority of the men and lead them yourself against the enemy cavalry, leaving perhaps a third to help the beleaguered warriors of the Spires at the stream (turn to **210**)?

161

It requires every ounce of your considerable strength to rip the emerald from its nesting-place in your face. Blood spurts, and you reel with pain. Part of the flesh of your cheek has been torn away in your sudden panic. You are now hideously disfigured; note that your face is horribly scarred. You pass a tormented night after the Palace physician leaves you, wondering what would have happened if you had left the Orb inside your head.

Turn to **131**.

162

'What are you doing here, then? There are plenty of priests among your legion,' says the officer. Then his eyes narrow, suspiciously. 'Or perhaps you are a spy. You had better come with me for questioning.' He signals to his men, some of whom rise up to approach you.

Will you try to make a run for it (turn to **202**) or attack the officer (turn to **212**)?

163

You decide to use your Sceptre as a staff on your journey. You have realised that you can use its effect of enhancing your charisma by merely wishing it. You travel to the Spires of Foreshadowing keeping well off the beaten track. There are no paved roads leading to Irsmuncast, but you stay well clear even of the beaten earth road that leads to the valley of the river Fortune. There are no signs of Honoric's troops being on the move yet, and you are reasonably sure that you haven't been followed when you finally join the road to the gates of the city. The spires of the temples stretch to awesome heights, each built to outdo the others and proclaim the importance of the god or goddess to whom it is dedicated. The city is bustling and seemingly full of well-to-do and powerful people. You decide to make for the tallest spire of all, that of the great hub-shaped Cathedral of Fate which dominates even this, the largest city in the Manmarch. Turn to **397**.

164

Instantly the cavalry, led by Toller, charges forwards, as do the Rangers. Happening and the other Tools are already moving to the danger point. Kelmic the Warrior is hurling fireballs and bolts of energy into the ranks of the enemy. Some get through, others are dispelled by the Legion's own spellcasters. The fighting is desperate.

Just then, three winged creatures, the Wyverns, flap up from behind Manor Ridge and streak towards the men of the Spires. The White Mage, high in the sky, his robes glittering in the sun, flies to meet them with bolts of lightning, words of power and potent magic. The Wyverns encircle him, lungeing with their jaws and whipping their poison-barbed tails.

Doré le Jeune gives a cry of, 'For Rocheval!', and he and his comrades race away to battle. Quickly you survey the rest of the field. The Levies on the left have not moved, but the Legion of the Angel of Death has charged in across the ford. The Legion is being held back but the legionaries seem to have no fear of death and keep on coming. The men of Fiendil are sorely beset – already their cavalry has charged in twice to throw back small breakthroughs. Will you send all your reserves to the far right of the field (turn to **184**) or lead the thousand men of Fiendil in reserve personally to the right flank and send Antocidas' men to the ford (turn to **194**)?

165

Flinging out your wings to their fullest extent and beating powerfully downwards, you rise up sharply. The ground falls away from you at a startling rate due to the innate magic of your hippogriff form. Shadazar tries to emulate you, but the dragon-vulture's body is too ponderous for her to mimic your manoeuvre and she sails beneath you, looking backwards and up at you over a scaly shoulder. Now you can attack her while she is vulnerable as she turns toward Cross Street. If you would like to dive on top of her, turn to **23**. If you would rather try to break her neck with your beak, turn to **47**.

166

You spur your horse forwards and Doré le Jeune accompanies you. Quickly you draw all your cavalry together on Colwyn's Mound and take up a position at the head. If you fought the duel with Honoric before the battle, turn to **96**. If you did not, turn to **226**.

167

There is an energetic debate after you have finished speaking. One of the followers of Dama says that the cause is a noble one and she calls upon the followers of Béatan to vote with them to become your ally. The head of the Boule, a learned man called Obuda Varhegyen, a follower of Béatan, commands rapt attention as he speaks, saying that to become your ally would be to strike a blow against law and that the rule of the war god would bring fatal stagnation and limitation of possibilities. The nature god's followers appear unconcerned, and the followers of Nemesis are against you: one says that to send forces as far away as the Manmarch is to invite attack by the Spawn of the Rift. When the vote is taken, however, it is marginally in your favour. You are asked to a meeting of the Boule leaders immediately after the other items of public business are settled. Turn to **227**.

168

Your horse prances wildly as the Old One closes in. Leaning out of the saddle, you whip your hand down at its head.

OLD ONE
Defence against Tiger's Paw chop: 7
Endurance: 22
Damage: 1 Die + 2

If you have killed it, turn to **198**. If it still lives, it swings its mace at your ribs. Your Defence is 7. If it hits you, take damage in the normal way and then turn to **208**. If it misses you, will you use the Tiger's Paw chop again (return to the top of this paragraph), spur your horse into it (turn to **188**) or hack at it with your Sceptre (turn to **178**)?

On the fifth day of Grimweird more information comes in from your scouts. Honoric has marched to a point just south of the City of Mortavalon and will be at the walls of Irsmuncast within a tenday. The Rift forces have split. The smaller force is veering west, apparently to join up with Honoric. The other, numbering at least ten thousand and perhaps many more, is marching directly on Irsmuncast and will arrive at the same time as Honoric's force. The carrion crows fly hither and thither over the city watching your preparations.

Glaivas suggests that you must try to defeat the enemy forces piecemeal, since together they outnumber you heavily. He suggests marching southwest to cut off the smaller force from the Rift to begin with. Antocidas suggests smashing the larger force, which would free more troops to march against Honoric later. If you do not, he says, then you will have to split efforts in two directions when the main mass of the enemy arrives. Gwyneth, however, would prefer to concentrate all your forces within the city and withstand a siege, attacking only when the enemy troops begin to fall out amongst themselves, which, she argues, is inevitable with such brutal creatures.

Whose advice will you follow, that of Glaivas (turn to **179**), Antocidas (turn to **209**) or Gwyneth (turn to **199**)?

At last the cavalry comes to your aid and the monks are driven back with heavy losses. Your decimated cavalry, still almost a thousand strong, rests nearby awaiting your orders. Then Doré le Jeune, his armour battered and stained with blood, rides up and shouts: 'We must have reinforcements at the stream, Overlord. The men of the Spires cannot hold out much longer.' You look to the left. Honoric's cavalry seems to have pulled back, but the Legion of the Sword of Doom is still trying to break through. However, the wooden walls of the farm and the stout defence of Gwyneth's warriors, the men of Fiendil and, surprisingly, Antocidas' mercenaries are holding them at bay. You notice that a thousand men from

Fiendil have not yet been committed there. Will you order your cavalry to charge into the fray at the stream (turn to **280**) or order the men at the farm to the stream and keep your cavalry back for now (turn to **290**)?

171

Cold panic grips you as you feel your flesh knitting around the Orb, which is soon firmly embedded in your eye socket. The emerald presses in, causing a sudden pain in your head, but this soon passes. Running your hands over your face you can feel that it has taken position just as if it were a translucent green eyeball. The severed muscles of the old eyeball regrow until you are surprised to realise that the green Orb moves in your head just as your real eye does. Then the whole world turns ghostly green. You are seeing through the Orb. Opening one eye at a time allows you to see a normal world or a green world of ghostly planes and visions which are superimposed upon reality. Note on your Character Sheet that you see through the Orb of Kings, and if you have played Book 4: *OVERLORD!* then restore your lost Modifiers. Turn to **191**.

172

You have just decided that there is little more you can learn when you come across an open clearing to the rear of the camp. Three huge wooden boxes with slat-like windows tightly closed are resting side by side. The boxes are reinforced with thick bands of iron and their doors are bolted shut with great iron bars. Strange shufflings and other indeterminable sounds emanate from the boxes. The Orb is glowing in your socket, most likely registering the presence of magic here. Will you examine the nearest box (turn to **192**) or decide that the whole thing is too dangerous and return to your own army (turn to **182**)?

The Cave Troll has begun swinging its great brazen club round and round its head, hoping to sweep you off your feet when it finally strikes home. You dart forwards and aim a straight-armed punch at its midriff.

CAVE TROLL
Defence against Iron Fist punch: 5
Endurance: 20
Damage: 2 Dice

If you have defeated the Cave Troll, turn to **19**. Otherwise the monster is now aiming a blow at your own midriff. Your Defence as you step aside is 8. If you are still alive you may counter with a Leaping Tiger kick (turn to **195**), a Whirlpool throw (turn to **155**) or punch again (return to the top of this paragraph).

As soon as they begin to fall back, the attackers redouble their efforts and the orderly withdrawal turns into a disorderly retreat, and then a full-scale rout. The Legion rushes forwards and then wheels around, its cavalry racing on to the ford. Soon the whole army is in full retreat. You are caught in the open, trying to rally your troops, by a squadron of the Bringers of Doom and slain out of hand.

The spider jumps on you at the last moment and you miss it with the sleeve iron. Tiny fangs break your skin and the poison courses through your veins. You die in seconds.

You had told the White Mage of what you had seen some hours earlier. Standing nearby, he says quietly, 'My time has come, Overlord,' and then he mutters something inaudible. Suddenly he takes to the air, to the astonishment of all those on Colwyn's Mound, and flies towards the Wickerwood. Just then three winged creatures, the Wyverns, flap up from behind Manor Ridge and streak towards the combined cavalry. The White Mage, high in the sky, his robes glittering in the sun, flies to meet them with bolts of lightning, words of power and potent magic. The Wyverns encircle him, lungeing with their jaws and whipping their poison-barbed tails.

Meanwhile, you raise the Sceptre high and cry, 'For Irsmuncast and freedom!' Doré le Jeune shouts, 'For Rocheval!' Your soldiers give a roar of approval and you charge forwards, 1,600 warriors at your back. The feeling is exhilarating as you race to battle wielding the Sceptre above your head.

Suddenly, in the midst of the battle a figure appears before you. Your Orb glows brightly – magic sight reveals that it is an Old One, perhaps the same one you fought when you strove for the Crown of Irsmuncast what seems like ages ago. From its robes protrude tentacles, and its mouth is rimmed with long tentacular appendages. One writhing 'hand' is curled around a heavy glowing mace. Those battling groups of warriors nearby back away, leaving a small arena.

'So, Avenger, you have come this far. But this is where your upstart reign ends,' it whispers sibilantly. You must fight it. You cannot kick or throw as you are on horseback, but you can use your mace-like Sceptre and your fists. Will you try a Tiger's Paw chop (turn to **168**), drive your Sceptre at it (turn to **178**) or spur your charger forwards and try to knock the Old One to the ground, (turn to **188**)? If you use the Sceptre to attack it, you cannot use Inner Force to double the damage.

177

The well-oiled doors to the Throne Room swing open soundlessly and you carry the Seneschal to a couch and lay him down before turning the great lock that seals the doors shut once more. There is the sound of orcish voices in the hallway outside as you cross the Throne Room to sit for a moment on your carven marble throne with its hippogriff shield. The Seneschal says, 'They will batter the doors down within minutes, Avenger. What is to be done?' You remember the secret passage by which you first entered this room to assassinate the evil Usurper. You tell the Seneschal that he is safe in your hands, then you ask him what has happened in the city.

Turn to **187**.

178

You hack down with your Sceptre. None of your Modifiers apply and you may not use Inner Force. If you hit the Old One, you will do 1 Die + 3 damage.

OLD ONE
Defence against Sceptre: 8
Endurance: 22
Damage: 1 Die +2

If you have killed it, turn to **198**. If it still lives, it swings its mace at your ribs. Your Defence is 7. If it hits you, take damage in the normal way and then turn to **208**. If it misses you, will you use the Sceptre again (return to the top of this paragraph), spur your horse into it (turn to **188**) or use a Tiger's Paw chop (turn to **168**)?

179

For the first time since your return, but not the last, you order the army into action. Gwyneth gifts you a magnificent white charger and you lead out your army to the southwest. The Rift forces turn south to avoid you, but your troops are faster than they are, and they number no more than six hundred, according to your scouts, so you order your cavalry to cut them off and annihilate them. When the cavalry return they report complete success. Those troops will not be reinforcing Honoric as they had hoped. They also carry tales of five fanatical knights wearing the red cross of Rocheval who appeared as if from nowhere to join in the carnage and then just as mysteriously rode away again. Note that you have prevented reinforcements from the Rift and turn to **269**.

You had told the White Mage of what you had seen some hours earlier. Standing nearby, he says quietly, 'My time has come, Overlord,' and then he mutters something inaudible. Suddenly he takes to the air, to the astonishment of all those on Colwyn's Mound, and flies towards the Wickerwood. Just then three winged creatures, the Wyverns, flap up from behind Manor Ridge and streak towards the men of the Spires. The White Mage, high in the sky, his robes glittering in the sun, flies to meet them with bolts of lightning, words of power and potent magic. The Wyverns encircle him, lungeing with their jaws and whipping their poison-barbed tails.

Meanwhile Doré le Jeune, to avoid the crossbow bolts, has led your cavalry back behind the men of the Spires, who have moved up to the ditch, using their shields to protect themselves from the bolts. Then the crossbowmen move aside, heading for Woodnugget Wood, presumably to try and flush out the Elves. The sound of eight thousand throats screaming a war-cry fills the air, and the men of the Spires, Aveneg and Mortavalon, the women of Horngroth and the Doomover Levies charge forwards at the worshippers of Fate, who hold the ditch. They crash into them with a resounding noise of steel upon steel, but the attackers cannot hold their impetus crossing the ditch and your men are able to keep them at bay. Turn to **200**.

Suddenly the invisible assassin takes shape before you. It slithers onwards on centipede's legs, but it is three metres tall. As it approaches, you make out a hideous human face with a gaping hole for a mouth surrounded by feeding tendrils. It has four arms and its body is that of a gigantic bloated centipede. A wicked scorpion's tail dangles a vicious poison barb just behind the awful head. You recognise it instantly as the most powerful and terrible monster you have ever had to face – Mardolh, one of the dreaded Sons of Nil, Mouth of the Void, the warped offspring of a god. You once banished it from this plane in the city of Harith on the Crow

River, but even with great skill and fortune you could not kill it. Will you throw yourself on the mercy of your god, Kwon the Redeemer, and pray (turn to **193**) or give battle even though to do so would seem hopeless (turn to **223**)?

182

'Discretion is the better part of valour,' you think to yourself as you steal through the camp and out into the night, back towards your own encampment. Turn to **100**.

183

The announcement of your imminent departure from Irsmuncast causes panic, but when you explain that you are going to find an ally who will help to protect the city, calm is restored. You declare a state of martial law and leave Force-Lady Gwyneth in charge, cautioning her to watch Lackland carefully but not to force any confrontation with the reverencers of Nemesis. To Lackland you say before you leave that you will fight for all the citizens and that the supporters of Nemesis will not suffer under your rule. After all, his forces outnumber Gwyneth's almost two to one. Antocidas is having a hard time stopping his mercenaries deserting, since there is precious little gold with which to pay them. In the interests of secrecy and quick movement you decide to travel to Serakub alone. Have you read the words of Nebr'Volent of the Eyeless Face? If so, turn to **53**. If not, turn to **27**.

184

You order your reserves into battle. Hastily they set off at a run. They reach the right flank just in time, as the tired defenders there are falling back. Suddenly the men of Fiendil at the ford waver and break, pursued by the Legion of the Angel of Death. The Levies charge across Ruric's Bridge to engage the women of Dama. The Legion of Vasch-Ro, from Aveneg and the Spires, and the spearmen of Mortavalon swing around to attack the rear of your right flank. Desperately you rush to the field to try to rally your men, but to no avail. Your men, trapped with you, fight

valiantly until, at last, only you and Doré le Jeune are left, fighting back to back. Such is your mutual prowess that Honoric orders his crossbowmen to pepper you both with bolts. 'Farewell, Avenger. You are a worthy warrior to die alongside,' are the Paladin's last words.

185

You carry on into the night, not resting until mid-morning the next day. When you awake a few hours later, the crows are wheeling far above your head once more. If you are making for Serakub, you must turn east (turn to **235**). If you are making for Greydawn, you head on due south (turn to **255**). In either case you have a long journey to make through rough wilderness, and the crows are watching you.

186

As you hurtle down Colwyn's Mound, three winged reptiles flap up above the Wickerwood. You recognise them as Wyverns, vicious creatures with poison-barbed tails and powerful jaws. They streak down to attack you. Instantly your charge is thrown into confusion as the horses, in terror, rear back uncontrollably, throwing off riders everywhere. You are struggling to control your horse when the great sting of a Wyvern's tail slams into your chest and you fly back through the air to fall in a heap, dead from the blow let alone from the effects of its virulent poison. Suddenly it is all over.

'After your departure, Overlord, the city was calm. As a tenday passed without word of you, those citizens who wished for a new Overlord started a rumour that you would never return, that you had gone to seek the Orb and Sceptre in the Rift and been swallowed up inside that evil place forever. Six days ago, news came that a new army of evil beings had issued forth from the Bowels of Orb to attack the city. Still there was no news of your majesty. The merchants fled the city, taking with them such wares as they could carry. The army and the militia, led by the Demagogue, manned the walls, but the black tide of evil swamped them this morning and great Cave Trolls breached the city wall. Orcs and Dark Elves led by some terrible sorcerous monster have taken much of the city and the eastern quarter burns. The temples on Cross Street still hold out and our forces have retreated to the Plaza of the Infinite Instant before the Temple to Time.' As he speaks there begins a loud battering on the doors to the Throne Room. At least you still have some troops left who may rally to your standard, but it will not be long before the doors cave in and you are both taken. Turn to **197**.

188

You try to spur your horse forwards, but it rears back in horror from contact with the strange creature, enabling the Old One to dart in and swing its mace at you. Your Defence is 7. If it hits you, the attack will deal 1 Die + 2 damage and then you must turn to **208**. If it misses you, will you try a Tiger's Paw chop (turn to **168**) or hack at it with your Sceptre (turn to **178**)?

189

The Seneschal seeks out a safer hiding place elsewhere as you leap down the staircase and turn the corner to the hallway outside the Throne Room. As you pass the great bronze doors, they shut with a click. You pause but have no time to find out who has just entered there as the hallway soon fills with Orcs from the far end. They shrink back before you. Something is wrong. They are not so much in fear of you as deferring to another being whose ponderous tread you now hear mounting the stairs towards the hallway. They pull back still further and a dark shadow looms up towards you. If you are skilled in Climbing and wish to retreat to the Palace roof and descend that way, turn to **393**. If you stand your ground ready to fight whatever may appear, turn to **385**.

190

Suddenly three winged creatures flap up into the air above the Wickerwood. You recognise them as Wyverns, evil creatures of great strength. They streak out of the sky at the cavalry near the stream. Simultaneously, the crossbowmen run forwards, fire, reload and run forwards again, firing on the run before turning away towards Woodnugget Wood, presumably to try to flush out the Elves. The Wyverns crash into the horsemen, lashing about with their tails and snapping jaws, causing havoc. Many die under the volley of bolts – there are more crossbowmen than cavalry. Then there is a guttural roar and Honoric's allies charge forwards. This is too much for your cavalry; despite Doré le Jeune, the men break and run, harried by the Wyverns that are killing indiscriminately.

You leap on to your horse to try to intercept the cavalry – you will have to rally it or the battle will be lost for sure. Then the White Mage, behind you, suddenly takes to the air, flying by some magical means. He engages the Wyverns, casting bolts of energy, words of power and other sorcerous weapons. The Wyverns flap upwards, forced to leave the fleeing horsemen to deal with the Mage.

The men of the Spires receive the charge of Honoric's allies and there is a resounding crash of steel on steel. Battle is joined, and the clash of weapons and the cries of the wounded fill the air – but your men are holding, just. Desperately, you canter off to meet the now decimated cavalry, which is set to flee off the field. On your far left the Legion of the Sword of Doom and its cavalry are charging the defenders at the farm repeatedly. The fighting is desperate, but your men look strong enough to hold on there for a little longer.

Towards you come the fleeing horsemen, some thousand left. You rein in your horse and raise your Sceptre high, calling on the power of the Sceptre, your false eye glowing with light. 'To me, warriors, to me. I can lead you to victory!' you cry. If you refused the challenge with Honoric before the battle, turn to **40**. If you accepted, turn to **50**.

191

The response to your new eye when you walk into the war council in the morning is dramatic. You certainly cut an imposing figure with your polished emerald eye that swivels in your head in time with your natural one. Turn to **131**.

192

You approach the nearest box. It is dark here, and no-one is about. The boxes seem unguarded save for a small unmarked tent nearby. Carefully you climb the side of the box, slide back one of the small windows and look inside. Three things happen simultaneously. You gasp in surprise at what you see inside: a huge reptilian beast – a Wyvern to be precise – a small patch of its iridescent scales glowing in the shaft of moonlight that streams in through the open window, lies asleep. The Orb seems to twitch as if some magic spell had been cast, and a great distant clanging fills the air – a magical alarm.

The Wyvern awakes, threshes its huge barbed tail and growls menacingly as you jump to the ground. Looking around, you see the immediate vicinity coming alive, and a man in robes, obviously a magician, erupts from the nearby tent, crying: 'The Wyverns, someone is at the Wyverns!' You have no choice but to try to escape. Turn to **202**.

193

Abandoning your self-reliance in the face of such a monster, you go down on one knee and call aloud to Kwon the Redeemer to help you. You sense Kwon's presence. He is watching over you in your hour of need, but he is not pleased. Subtract 2 points from your current Inner Force. It seems that even your god may be withdrawing his support. But then his voice fills your brain. 'Your foe is no demi-god.' Kwon's presence leaves you just as one of Mardolh's arms smashes into your side. Lose 3 Endurance. If you are still alive, you will have to fight. Turn to **223**.

194

A Wyvern plummets from the sky and you look up. Two of the winged beasts are left, although the White Mage's robes are spattered with red. You rush down the Greenridge to take control of the reserve. Hengist and his men accompany you. Quickly you shout at Antocidas: 'Take your men to the ford and hold it!' But he only eyes you evenly. 'Another talent when we get home, my lord, or my men don't fight.' It is all you can do to smother your rage. A talent is the weight of a man in pure gold, the currency with which a city is run. Will you refuse point blank and order the cavalry of Dama on the far left to the ford (turn to **204**) or sullenly agree (turn to **214**)?

195

The great grey Cave Troll sneers at you and shakes its club. The club's black spikes are already dripping with blood which the Troll wishes to mix with your own. As it tries to smash you, you leap high and drive the ball of your foot towards its chest. But the Troll's reach is long and it may catch you with the club.

CAVE TROLL
Defence against Leaping Tiger kick: 7
Endurance: 20
Damage: 2 Dice

If you have defeated the Cave Troll, turn to **19**. Otherwise the Troll lumbers forwards and tries a cunningly low sweep with its club designed to knock your legs from under you. Your Defence against this whistling blow as you leap high to avoid it is 6. If you are still alive you may use the Iron Fist punch (turn to **173**), the Whirlpool throw (turn to **155**) or the Leaping Tiger kick once more (return to the top of this paragraph).

196

You charge forwards to battle, but while you are driving off the rest of Honoric's cavalry the battle is lost behind you. The swordsmen cannot move fast enough and your whole left flank is overrun by the Legion of the Sword of Doom, who begin to mop up the rest of your forces piecemeal. You try to ride off the field, but your men are caught in a volley of crossbow fire, and a bolt takes you in your eye, forcing the Orb backwards into your brain and killing you instantly.

197

The Seneschal rises from the couch and you make for the secret doorway that connects the Throne Room to the dungeons beneath the Palace. Suddenly the Sceptre seems almost to tug itself out of your grasp. Will you tie it to your costume and leave the Throne Room (turn to **299**) or stay and take the time to examine it (turn to **311**)?

198

Your last blow caves in the thing's skull and it falls dead. If your allies are the worshippers of Fate from the Spires of Foreshadowing and from Fiendil, turn to **66**. If not, read on. If your original plan was to defend all along the stream (using the map at **24**), turn to **248**. If your original plan was to refuse the left flank (using the map at **14**), turn to **6**. If your original plan was to refuse the right flank (using the map at **34**), turn to **16**.

Your allies grumble that they did not come all this way to be
trapped bottled up inside a city, but you back Gwyneth's
decision staunchly. A tenday later the two enemy forces
unite around the city walls and you wait for the bickering to
begin. Unfortunately, something that you could not have
foreseen renders your strategy misguided. The forces of the
Rift are commanded by an Old One who is able to keep the
troops disciplined, and the uneasy truce outside the gates
lasts too long. At last you are forced to sally out due to lack
of food, and their combined forces overwhelm you. You die
defending the city to the last.

You can see Doré le Jeune fighting with the men of the
Spires, defending the ditch bravely. Suddenly there are cries
of alarm. From the Old Farm come two hundred monks of
the Scarlet Mantis pounding up the hill to your position.
'They must have come from the Wickerwood!' cries Hengist,
as he and his fellows crowd around you. The Corps of
Bannermen surround you as the monks, in unnerving
silence, fall upon your position. Already the cavalry is
coming to your aid, but the monks seem intent on only one
thing, getting to you and killing you.

Suddenly a man breaks through to face you. Your Orb
glows brightly – magic sight reveals that it is an Old One,
perhaps the same one you fought when you strove for the
Crown of Irsmuncast what seems like ages ago. From its
robes protrude tentacles, and its mouth is rimmed with long
tentacular appendages. One writhing 'hand' is curled around
a heavy glowing mace. Those battling groups of warriors
nearby back away, leaving a small arena.

'So, Avenger, you have come this far. But this is where
your upstart reign ends,' it whispers sibilantly.

You must fight it. You cannot kick or throw as you are on
horseback, but you can use your mace-like Sceptre and your
fists.

Will you try a Tiger's Paw chop (turn to **60**), drive your
Sceptre at it (turn to **70**) or spur your charger forwards and

try to knock the Old One to the ground (turn to **80**)? If you use the Sceptre to attack it, you cannot use Inner Force to double the damage.

Throughout these troubled times Onikaba and his hundred samurai have remained courageous and loyal. They have suffered some losses but Onikaba has recruited and trained people from the city to replace those killed or wounded. If only, you think, you had a thousand such troops. But there is no time to send for help to the Island of Plenty, and it would never arrive in time. Then when Onikaba dies suddenly of a heart attack, his men ask to be allowed home. They have served you so well that you decide you must let them go. Turn to **221**.

You turn tail and flee, but the alarm is raised. You run through the darkness using all your skills to avoid groups of blundering searchers. Then, directly ahead of you, a line of legionaries appears in the gloom. They are being marshalled in to order by several officers prior to beginning a systematic search. Will you run straight at them (turn to **222**), break off and cut to the left (turn to **232**) or duck into the nearest tent (turn to **242**)?

As night approaches, one of the carrion crows caws faintly and then lets itself be borne away by the wind in the direction of the Rift. Long before the last light has gone, your acute sense of smell alerts you to something unnatural. All is peculiarly still, the wind has changed and the taint on the air is coming from the direction of the Rift. The world goes a glassy green. For some reason your brain is concentrating on the vision it receives from the emerald Orb. You recoil in shock. Just a few paces away from you is a creature from your worst nightmares. Its body is like that of a six-legged mammoth from which the flesh has wasted away. It has three heads, each totally different and each overloaded with

a fearsome array of tusks, fangs and horns. Its shape shifts as if it moved by floating, its feet not quite in contact with the bare earth. You can see nothing through your natural eye; the creature is invisible to normal men. Three misshapen serrated tongues slaver and saw at grotesquely calloused lips. Its intention — to kill you – cannot be mistaken. It towers high above you. Will you use the Forked Lightning kick (turn to **213**), the Cobra Strike punch (turn to **263**) or the Winged Horse kick (turn to **283**)?

(turn to **213**) ... (turn to **263**) ... (turn to **283**)

204

As you lead the reserve to the right flank, Antocidas' men begin to march off the field. As soon as the Cavalry of Doom moves towards the ford, the Doomover Levies charge the bridge. They are hacked down in droves by the women of Serakub, but they do not fall back, as the Warrior Women of Fell-Kyrinla also hack down any who retreat. Casualties among the women of Dama mount slowly.

The crossbowmen have entered Woodnugget Wood and the Elves are forced to break off their withering fire to deal with the Legion. The men assaulting the ford redouble their efforts. Suddenly, before the cavalry of Dama has even crossed the Old Bridge, the men of Fiendil break and run, pursued closely by the Legion of the Angel of Death, depleted though it is.

You ride into battle, but it is not long before your position has been attacked in the rear by the Vasch-Ro legionaries of the Spires, Mortavalon and Aveneg and the Legion of the Angel of Death. Your men, trapped with you, fight valiantly until, at last, only you and Doré le Jeune are left, fighting back to back. Such is your mutual prowess that Honoric orders his crossbowmen to pepper you both with bolts. 'Farewell, Avenger. You are a worthy warrior to die alongside,' are the Paladin's last words.

205

As you step back there is a sharp pain in your heel: you have trodden on one of the executioner spiders. Tiny fangs pump poison into your body. Death is mercifully swift. Now

Honoric and the forces from the Rift will carve up the fate of Irsmuncast between them.

206

As you gallop at breakneck speed with about nine hundred surviving horsewomen of Dama behind you, you catch sight of the White Mage up above. He has slain all three Wyverns but is himself drenched in blood, barely alive. Just as Honoric's allies are about to fall on the rear of Antocidas' mercenaries, you charge home, scattering soldiers before you. The sight of you, your Orb and Sceptre, Doré le Jeune and the formidable warriors of Dama is too much for the attackers, and they are forced, back, despite their numbers. By the time they are ready to attack once more, Gwyneth's swordswomen have secured the Greenridge, presenting an indomitable array of warriors.

Meanwhile, Honoric's remaining cavalry has been repulsed by the Warrior Women of Serakub once more and the men are in full retreat, this time unable to regroup. Turn to **216**.

207

After your speech there follows an energetic debate. It appears that some at least of the followers of Dama wish to ally with you. The followers of Béatan are split and the followers of the nature god indifferent, while the followers of Nemesis and Nullaq are against you. As they are about to take the vote, you sense that something you say now could swing the vote one way or another . Will you say that you will come to their aid, if ever they are attacked (turn to **277**) or mention that you are in the middle of a campaign against the Spawn of the Rift was well (turn to **307**)?

208

As the blow connects, you feel a surge of sorcerous energy that emanates from the black glowing mace threatening to engulf you. Make a Fate Roll, but apply −2 to your Fate Modifier for this roll only. If Fate smiles on you, turn to **218**. If Fate turns her back on you, turn to **228**.

With a great parade and much tearful leave-taking, you lead out your army in full panoply of war. Gwyneth gifts you a magnificent white charger, and you cut a right royal dash riding out at the head of your troops with your Sceptre and your glowing green emerald eye. Unfortunately, the crow scouts of your enemy see you coming and the Rift forces draw back even as Honoric advances from the other direction. You cannot chase them down into the Bowels of Orb, for your troops would be hopelessly disadvantaged in the maze of catacombs and caverns in the Rift. Honoric, however, will never retreat, regarding it as dishonourable. You return and hold a final council of war, where you decide to concentrate on his forces alone. Your troops rest in Irsmuncast for one last night. Turn to **239**.

Quickly you shout orders and call Doré le Jeune to your side. Up above, the White Mage has slain all the Wyverns, but the price is high. He floats earthwards, his white robes splashed with crimson, his face a contorted mask of pain. He may yet live.

Then, raising your Sceptre high above your head, you cry, 'To battle! For Irsmuncast and freedom for all!' Doré le Jeune shouts, 'For Rocheval!', and the men and women behind you, surging forwards, give a great shout of, 'Avenger!' You are filled with exhilaration as you charge forwards, a thousand or more warriors at your back. Ahead of you, another line of black-clad horsemen races to meet you.

The impact is shattering as the two lines meet. You find yourself face to face with a Worshipper of Death, a captain of the Wings of Death. You despatch him quickly. Beside you, Doré le Jeune and his Paladins are like a tornado, laying about to terrible effect. What follows is a whirling, running battle that seems to end as suddenly as it began. Honoric's cavalry is retreating fast, though in good order. You have led your cavalry to victory. It was your presence, and that of Doré le Jeune, which gave the men that extra vitality. But

they are badly mauled. Some way off, the enemy horsemen, bullied by their officers, are regrouping for another charge. Looking back, you see that your men at the stream have been forced back to Colwyn's Mound. The battle hangs in the balance. Will you lead your cavalry back to charge the Doomover Levies and Honoric's allies in the flank (turn to **220**) or pursue the cavalry ahead of you to finish it off (turn to **230**)?

211

The grey-skinned Troll lumbers forwards, brandishing its great club. It is about three metres tall and almost as broad as the doors to the Throne Room. You wait motionless as if paralysed with fear until it is about to strike. Then in a blur of movement you whirl like an uncoiling spring and lash out a devastatingly powerful Kwon's Flail kick at the surprised beast.

CAVE TROLL
Defence against Kwon's Flail kick: 6
Endurance: 20
Damage: 2 Dice

If you have defeated the Cave Troll, turn to **19**. If it still lives, you must now avoid a great sweep of its spiked club. Your Defence as you dodge its cumbersome blow is 5. If you are still alive, you cannot practically use Kwon's Flail again in such quarters and may now use the Leaping Tiger kick (turn to **195**), the Iron Fist punch (turn to **173**) or the Whirlpool throw (turn to **155**).

212

You lash out at the officer, and he falls back stunned. The soldiers rush at you, drawing their swords. You fight valiantly, but you are in the middle of Honoric's army. It is only a matter of time before you are overwhelmed and slain.

213

The monster appears not to notice your feint. It is trying to bite, gore or rake you with each one of its heads. You may not block as you try to dodge rather than defend yourself against it.

THE SPAWN OF THE RIFT
Defence against Forked Lightning kick: 4
Endurance: 24
Damage: 2 Dice + 3

If you win, turn to **323**. Otherwise your Defence against its three-pronged attack is only 6. If you survive, you may try the same move again (return to the top of this paragraph), try the Winged Horse kick (turn to **283**) or the Cobra Strike punch (turn to **263**).

214

Antocidas leads his men to the ford, where they arrive just in time to prevent a major breakthrough. You lead the reserve at a run to the right flank, where the men of the Spires are giving ground rapidly, poised to break and run at any moment. You charge into the fray on your white charger, wielding the Sceptre. If you refused the challenge of single combat with Honoric, turn to **224**. If you fought him, turn to **234**.

215

You may have cause to thank Kwon for your training. One of the poisons used in this training is the venom of the executioner spider, but this is so virulent that you have never been able to take more than a diluted droplet without falling unconscious. Make a note of the number **225** and, if you are bitten by only a single spider, turn to that paragraph. Now turn to **373** and make your choice.

216

Quickly you lead your still formidable cavalry force and the Warrior Women of Irsmuncast to fall on the left flank of the Legion of the Sword of Doom. Sensing the taste of victory, the rest of your army moves to the offensive. Soon the whole of Honoric's army is in full retreat with the Doomover Levies completely routed and fleeing pell-mell. Your forces are relatively well off – some elements are too exhausted, such as the defenders at the farm, but you begin issuing orders for those still able to go on. Note that you are able to carry out a pursuit. Turn to **250**.

217

After you have finished speaking there is an energetic debate. One of the followers of Dama says that yours is a just and noble cause and calls upon the followers of Béatan to vote with her and become your ally. The followers of Béatan appear to be divided, and the followers of the nature god indifferent. Those of Nemesis claim that to send forces to your aid would leave the city exposed to an attack by the Spawn of the Rift. Suddenly a priestess of Nullaq, the Supreme Queen who rules in Malicious Envy and whose Touch is Poison, stands up and denounces you as a trickster who uses magic to beguile the members of the Boule. Will you admit that you have used the power of the Sceptre (turn to **237**) or ignore her, saying instead that you are also in the middle of a war with the Spawn of the Rift (turn to **287**), or say that you will promise under threat of a dire curse to come to their aid if they are ever attacked (turn to **377**)?

218

You manage to overthrow whatever magical force threatened you. The Old One growls in frustration. Will you try a Tiger's Paw chop (turn to **168**), hack at it with your Sceptre (turn to **178**) or spur your horse forwards into the Old One (turn to **188**)?

You decide to use your Sceptre as a staff on your journey. You come to realise it has special power, where just by wishing to, you can influence people who are not already hostile to you. You travel to the Spires of Foreshadowing keeping well off the beaten track. There are no paved roads leading to Irsmuncast, but you stay well clear even of the beaten earth road that leads to the valley of the river Fortune. There are no signs of Honoric's troops being on the move yet, and you are reasonably sure that you haven't been followed when you finally join the road to the gates of the city. The spires of the temples stretch to awesome heights, each built to outdo the others and proclaim the importance of the god or goddess to whom it is dedicated. The city is bustling and seemingly full of well-to-do and powerful people. You decide to make for the tallest spire of all, that of the great hub-shaped Cathedral of Fate which dominates even this, the largest city in the Manmarch. Turn to **397**.

You race back at the head of your cavalry and wheel around into the flank of the Doomover Levies. Almost simultaneously, you see the crossbowmen retreating from Woodnugget Wood. Gliftel's Elves, even outnumbered ten to one, have managed to throw them out of the wood, the Elves' natural element. Your cavalry with you, Doré le Jeune and his Paladins cut through the ill-trained Levies like a knife through butter, scattering them before you. A few minutes later, they break and flee. The hard-pressed men of the Spires, sensing victory, fight back with new strength, and soon all Honoric's men on that flank are in full flight. The men of the Spires are simply too exhausted to pursue. Those still alive can barely stand from fatigue. You exhort the remnants of your cavalry to one more effort and wheel back to support your men at the farm. However, to your joy, the Legion of the Sword of Doom and the shattered cavalry are beginning a complete retreat. Note that you are unable to pursue the enemy. Turn to **250**.

Gwyneth reports that her scouts have watched Shadazar's army, which, though beaten, was not pursued from the city, and has now returned to the Bowels of Orb. Though lacking a leader, they suffered only small losses when taking and being driven from the city. 'There is no telling when the Spawn of the Rift will issue forth again from the dark places beneath Orb,' says Gwyneth. 'Indeed, Fate would truly be smiling on us if they did not attack us again when their carrion crows carry the news of the advance of the Legion of the Sword of Doom.' Even the Demagogue agrees with everyone that you lack the forces necessary to hope for success. Solstice, the saturnine High Priest of the powerful Templars to Time, has said nothing yet Will you ask him to send spell-casters to help your army (turn to **241**) or ignore him (turn to **301**)?

You sprint directly at the line of approaching soldiers, the nearest of whom stares at you in puzzlement. Will you try to smash your way through them (turn to **322**) or shout: 'Hey, lads, what's going on?' (turn to **332**)?

As Mardolh lurches forwards to strike, you have time only to duck and drive a Cobra Strike punch below the studded leather belt that covers the divide between his human torso and the bloated centipede body. Mardolh's Defence is 6. If you have struck successfully, turn to **231**. If not, you are caught by one of the four pounding fists. Lose 3 Endurance and, if you still live, return to the top of this paragraph.

Despite your presence with the Sceptre and the arrival of fresh troops, the beleaguered warriors' flagging morale is not uplifted. You sense that the rank and file have lost confidence in you for refusing to accept the duel with Honoric. They were prepared to fight for you, but you were not prepared to fight for them. A fresh charge by Honoric's cavalry seals your fate and the right flank breaks and runs, closely followed by the rest of your line. A rout ensues, followed by a slaughter as the cavalry pursues. You attempt to rally your men, but are cut down almost incidentally by the heavy cavalry of the Bringers of Doom. Perhaps you will be remembered in a song.

225

The poison courses through your veins, but your immunity lessens the effect of the venom of the executioner spider. You lose 8 Endurance, however, before you have smashed the last of the spiders to a messy pulp. If you are still alive, you can hardly believe your eyes when the Dark Elves remount the giant carrion crows, which then flap away into the gathering dusk that seems to flow out of the Rift like a black mist. Turn to **185**.

226

You give a battle-cry as you lead the charge, but the response from your warriors is muted, despite the effects of the Sceptre. It seems they have lost confidence in you. You charge forwards, but the warriors of Horngroth wheel to meet you head on. Your charge seems ineffectual. It is almost as if your presence is having an adverse effect on their morale. The charge is repulsed, and Honoric's cavalry unleashes another charge and this time breaks through to fall upon the rear of your left flank. Within half an hour your whole army is in full rout. You try to ride off the field, but your men are caught in a volley of crossbow fire and a bolt takes you in your eye, forcing the Orb backwards into your brain and killing you instantly.

227

While you wait in the smaller council chamber, the Prodromese are debating about how many troops to send to your aid. At last the door opens and two people enter. The first is the learned head of the Boule, Obuda Varhegyen, dressed in a long yellow robe bearing the five arrowed half-wheels that signify the many ways to do good deeds, central

to the theology of Béatan. Behind him is a most striking woman wearing a plain kirtle and a blue shawl, her coppery hair done up in silk twists. Her blue eyes are warm and soft and she smiles as Obuda introduces her as Hivatala, the Swordsmistress of the Serakub Guard. Your surprise at her title is obvious, and this pleases her. You sit around a small table and they tell you what has passed in the Boule. Only two thousand troops have been voted to help you in the campaign, but Hivatala says that she will call for volunteers to augment this. Obuda also feels that the followers of Béatan at the City of Aveneg in the Manmarch are sure to send men if he sends a message to them, for they are strongly opposed to Honoric. By the time you leave the pleasant City of Gardens, you are beginning to feel that there is hope. Hivatala herself will command the forces of Serakub, and she will arrive with two thousand shieldmaidens, including five hundred mounted troops, along with a thousand swordsmen of the Army of Myriad Possibility, followers of Béatan. Turn to **387**.

228

You feel a cold numbing in your very soul – some part of you has been sucked into the mace. If you have no points of Inner Force left, turn to **334**. Otherwise, lose 1 point of Inner Force. Will you try a Tiger's Paw chop (turn to **168**), hack at the Old One with your Sceptre (turn to **178**) or spur your horse forwards in an attempt to knock the Old One over (turn to **188**)?

229

Early the next morning a messenger comes to the Royal bedchamber. If you have played Book 3: *USURPER!* and a Paladin called Doré le Jeune helped you to defeat the Usurper when you toppled him from the throne, turn to **249**. Otherwise turn to **259**.

230

You give the order and gallop forwards, flushed with the taste of victory. Your cavalry surges after, Doré le Jeune shouting gleefully. A fight to the death ensues, with your men getting the better of it. Honoric's cavalry is fighting desperately. It is only the Bringers of Doom that are holding it together. However, behind you the men of the Spires can take no more. They break and run in full retreat. The Doomover Levies stream after them, but the regular soldiers of Horngroth, Mortavalon and Aveneg swing left into the back of your men holding the farm.

The battle is lost. The men at and around the farm are virtually annihilated. Finally a lance takes you in the throat as you try to rally your men and you are slain.

231

Surprisingly, your blow causes the enormous Son of Nil to convulse and slither backwards. Then he seems to collapse in on himself like a shrinking balloon and change colour until he is black all over. When the process is complete you see before you not a Son of Nil but a Vulcan Imp, a being from the lower planes, the Seven Hells or the many layers of the Abyss. Such beings are able to reach into men's minds and dredge forth images of fear from the memory. The Imp only appeared as Mardolh, but your problems are not yet over. It grins malevolently and its skin begins to smoke. Soon the clouds of smoke will have completely obscured it and it will attack again. Will you return to the Throne Room (turn to **245**) or risk everything in a reckless attack into the smoke (turn to **257**)?

232

You sprint away, avoiding all areas of illumination. You make it to the edge of the camp, but suddenly a large misshapen creature looms up in front of you. It is an Ogre, grotesquely dressed as a soldier of Doomover. It growls menacingly as you approach. If you have the skill of Acrobatics, turn to **282**. If not, turn to **292**.

233

As you leap down the staircase and turn the corner to the hallway outside the Throne Room, a host of Orcs shrink back before you. But something is wrong. They are not so much in fear of you as deferring to another being whose ponderous tread you now hear mounting the stairs towards the hallway. They pull back still further and a dark shadow looms up towards you. If you would like to retreat to the Palace roof and, if you are skilled at Climbing, descend that way, turn to **393**. If you stand your ground, ready to fight whatever may appear, turn to **385**.

234

At the sight of you and the effects of the Sceptre, the defenders give a great shout of joy. Your fresh troops crash into battle. You, Doré le Jeune and his Paladins, and Hengist rally the 350-or-so-strong Spires cavalry and lead a charge. Morale high, and with some of the finest warriors on the field at their head, they crash into the cavalry of the Wings of Death. The fight is short and bitter and the enemy is decimated, Doré le Jeune striking to left and right like a man possessed. They break and flee, taking many of the cavalry of Horngroth with them. Up above, the White Mage has slain all three Wyverns, although he is forced to retire to the Greenridge, almost dead himself.

Suddenly, in the midst of the battle, a figure appears before you. Your Orb glows brightly – magic sight reveals that it is an Old One, perhaps the same one you fought when you strove for the Crown of Irsmuncast what seems like ages ago. From its robes protrude tentacles, and its mouth is rimmed with long tentacular appendages. One writhing 'hand' is curled around a heavy glowing mace. Those battling groups of warriors nearby back away, leaving a small arena.

'So, Avenger, you have come this far. But this is where your upstart reign ends,' it whispers sibilantly. You must fight it. You cannot kick or throw as you are on horseback, but you can use your mace-like Sceptre and your fists. Will you try a Tiger's Paw chop (turn to **264**), drive your Sceptre at it (turn to **274**) or spur your charger forwards and try to knock the Old One to the ground (turn to **284**)? If you use the Sceptre to attack it, you cannot use Inner Force to double the damage.

Your stealth and such woodcraft as you have, in particular your skill as a tracker, are put to good use as you turn eastwards through the wilderness. Several times you almost run into warbands of Orcs returning from raiding across the plain of the Inner Sea. Evidently Irsmuncast is not the only city that suffers at the hands of the Spawn of the Rift. You are still two days out of Serakub, skirting the Deeping Woods, when a party of twenty riders emerges from the forest and gallops towards you. You are relieved to see that they carry the familiar lozenge-shaped shields of followers of Dama. It is a patrol from the city of Serakub. Turn to **17**.

As your cavalry surges forwards, Honoric's reacts with drill-like precision. The cavalry splits apart and the crossbowmen, the Rain of Doom, run forwards to unleash a devastating volley of crossbow bolts. It is as if your cavalry had run into a brick wall, the front ranks dropping in a tangled heap of horses and men. Then the enemy cavalry closes in again on your disordered horsemen. The carnage is terrible. Half your cavalry is slain in minutes and the rest streams off the battlefield, utterly routed. The battle is over virtually before it has begun. The Legion of the Sword of Doom is able to pick and choose where to attack through the huge gaps in your defences, and it is not long before the rest of your army is on the run. You are cut down trying to rally your troops, killed almost in passing by a squadron of cavalrymen.

'What naked admission of guilt is this?' cries a follower of Nemesis. The followers of Dama turn away from you. Only the followers of Béatan seem unperturbed, and one argues that the facts remain as they are stated. But the vote goes heavily against you. Obuda Varhegyen, the head of the Boule, says that you will find no alliance with the people of Serakub. You return forthwith to see to the defence of Irsmuncast, but when Honoric attacks your forces are overwhelmed and you die defending the walls.

Gwyneth stands and says, 'First let us hear the reports of our scouts,' and she indicates Glaivas. Glaivas says, 'This is what we can determine of Honoric's forces,' and reads out a report. He then hands it to you.

THE ARMY OF HONORIC

Legion of the Sword of Doom	5,000 swordsmen
	2,000 crossbowmen, the Rain of Doom
	500 cavalry (Cataphracts), the Bringers of Doom
Legion of Aveneg	1,000 swordsmen
Legion of the Spires	1,000 swordsmen
Women of Horngroth	1,000 swordswomen
	500 cavalry
Men of Mortavalon	1,000 spearmen of Moraine
Monks of the Scarlet Mantis	200
Doomover Levies	4,000
A total of some	16,200 troops

'We can field about 8,000 men, heavily outnumbered. And the Legion of the Sword of Doom are reckoned to be the best in all the Manmarch,' adds Glaivas.

Turn to **4**.

That evening, Greystaff, the High Priest of the Temple to Avatar, introduces to you a man he calls the White Mage. He wears a white robe and the tall conical hat worn by wizards only in fairy tales, but if Greystaff says you should let him join the army, you reflect, you will be only too glad to agree. Turn to **229**.

Your cavalry charges bravely to meet them. There is a terrible crash as they come together and many are killed from the impact. Minutes later the men at the stream, outnumbered two to one and driven slowly back, finally break and run. They stream past your position, hotly pursued. At this, your army's morale gives out, your forces begin to break up. Desperately you try to rally some men for a final stand, but to no avail. At the end you are slain by a group of Cataphracts, who do not even know who you are. Perhaps you will be remembered in a song, somewhere.

'The trials and tribulations of the rulers of cities are beneath the notice of the Temple of the Snowfather, who came before all and will endure after all, just as the Temple to the Seasons would survive under the rule of the one you call Honoric,' replies Solsti

'And under the Spawn of the Rift?' queries the Demagogue. 'Even you, Solstice, who closets himself away from the world must have heard the tales of the City of Bone that lies deep below the Rift. How would your precious Temple fare under the rule of the Old Ones?'

Solstice is unmoved by the Demagogue's outburst. There will be no help promised from the Temple to Time. Turn to **301**.

You burst into a tent. Inside, a soldier with a bowl of steaming broth in front of him gawps at you in astonishment. Quickly you leave with a muttered apology. A long line of soldiers is moving towards you. Nearby, a cart loaded with weapons and other gear rests next to a large siege engine. Will you dart into the shadows of the engine (turn to **252**), run to the left as fast as you can (turn to **232**) or run straight at the line of warriors (turn to **222**)?

243

Do you see through the Orb of Kings? If you do, turn to **203**. If not, turn to **253**.

244

Instantly the cavalry, led by Toller, charges forwards, as do the Rangers. Happening and the other Tools are already moving to the danger point, Kelmic the Warrior hurling fireballs and bolts of energy into the ranks of the enemy. Some get through, others are dispelled by the Legion's own spellcasters. The fighting is desperate.

Just then three winged creatures, flying reptiles, flap up from behind Manor Ridge. To your horror, you recognise them. They are Wyverns. They streak to the attack, wreaking terrible devastation on the soldiers on the ground with their jaws and poison-barbed tails. Within seconds, before you have time even to issue orders, your whole right flank crumbles and flees in terror.

Honoric's cavalry pursues relentlessly, slaughtering the remnants of the men from the Spires. The Legion of the Sword of Doom advances to swing around at the ford's defenders. Minutes later, Antocidas and his men flee the field without even having struck a blow. Doré le Jeune rides into the fray, but it is hopeless. You try to rally your men, but the whole army is fleeing in disorder. You find yourself cut off and isolated, to be cut down alone and without friends on the battlefield. Perhaps you will be remembered in a song.

245

At the stairhead you pull the torch bracket which swings open the secret door into the Throne Room and then you leap inside, surprising a sea of Orcs and two great Trolls. They were intent on looting the room's rich trappings of majesty, but now their attention is turned to you. You realise that you will never reach the door so you try to return to the dungeon. To your dismay the secret door swings shut and try as you might you cannot open it. The demonic laughter of the Imp tells you that it is swinging from the bracket, trapping you. You fight heroically, but at length you are overwhelmed and slain in your own Throne Room.

246

Hurriedly the men of Aveneg rush into position as the cavalry, led by the Bringers of Doom, clad from head to toe in gleaming steel, slams into the attack. Your men reel back with the shock but they manage to hold on. The Rain of Doom move off to the side, facing Woodnugget Wood, while the Legion itself follows close behind the cavalry.

Honoric's cavalry is flung back, but then the infantry charges in and a vicious head-to-head mêlée begins. The fighting is particularly bitter at Hartwig Fell's Farm, where a staunch defence is going on from behind the wooden fences. But the men strung out between the farm and Tallhill are threatened under the onslaught. Will you ask the cavalry of Serakub and Irsmuncast to charge around the farm at the Legion (turn to **256**) or order the warriors of Aveneg at Tallhill to swing in at the Legion (turn to **266**)?

247

You sprint to the edge of the Palace roof and peer over the battlements to the gardens below. The smoke thins to reveal a sea of brutish Orc faces looking up expectantly. There is no escape that way, so you descend the stairs which lead toward the Throne Room. In the hallway outside the great bronze doors a host of Orcs is lined up behind a great grey-skinned Cave Troll, three metres tall, who had been about to climb the stairs when you appeared. It sneers horribly, shaking a huge brazen club with black spikes. There is no time to think. Will you use the Leaping Tiger kick (turn to **195**), the Iron Fist punch (turn to **173**) or the Whirlpool throw (turn to **155**)?

The Old One lies at your horse's feet. You look up from your struggle to a glorious sight. The opposing cavalry has been driven off and is in retreat, falling back in good order. Your presence and the presence of Doré le Jeune, who fights like a whirlwind, was enough to give your soldiers the edge over the élite Bringers of Doom. But casualties have been heavy on both sides. Turn to **7**.

The message is that a Paladin from Beyond the Rift called Doré le Jeune and four companions, all of whom wear the red cross of Rocheval, Prince of Knights Errant, Wielder of the Holy of Holies, are requesting permission to join your army. You leap out of bed and pull on your clothes, eager to greet that great warrior who helped at your time of need, forgetful for the moment of the great zeal that drove him to the ends of Orb in a single-handed attempt to eradicate evil from existence. He is pleased to see you, and you say that you will be honoured to have him and his friends ride beside you. You ask him why he left without a word, and he replies: 'There was more evil without Irsmuncast than within. Besides, I left you behind to take care of things.' You retort that things seem to be taking care of you since he left and he smiles. Turn to **309**.

In the distance you recognise Honoric himself on horseback trying to whip the remnants of his army into good enough shape for a safe withdrawal. But then he puts something to his lips and blows. It is a horn. A great, echoing blast of sound fills the heavens, seeming to echo across all the planes of existence. Your heart and the hearts of your army quail with fear. Doré le Jeune claps his hands over his ears. Then something begins to materialise in front of Honoric. A huge Colossus, eight metres tall and ebony black, appears. In its hand it wields a huge sword, the mirror of Honoric's eldritch blade Sorcerak, but many times larger. The black titan, eyes aglow with lambent fire, lumbers towards you, an aura of pale nacreous light playing about its limbs. Will you ask Doré le Jeune to accompany you, and whatever cavalry you have available, to charge once more (turn to **376**) or order your men to fall back before the monster (turn to **386**)?

251

'Then where would you have me go, Antocidas?' you enquire of the burly mercenary.

'Greydawn,' he answers. The others look up in surprise. 'The forces of Moraine, God of Empire, are ever seeking an excuse for battle. They live only to fight, and half their troops, it is said, are not men at all but beastlings, each as strong as two men.'

Greystaff says: 'Might we not find that we had brought an even greater evil into the Manmarch?'

Antocidas replies: 'We could bribe them with land to the east of our city. They would protect us from the Spawn of the Rift then. Irsmuncast has always suffered because it is the easternmost city of the Manmarch, nearest the Bowels of Orb.'

Turn to **361**.

252

You crouch hidden, your breathing as quiet as the grave and your body unmoving. The line of searchers passes past you without finding you. You wait for the furore to die down, and you are just thinking it is safe to come out when a sound alerts you. Suddenly the Orb glows. Then somebody nearby gasps in surprise and you realise a magician has used magic to find you. You leap up and a young sorcerer, of Nemesis it would seem, stands before you, momentarily surprised. You must silence him before he gives the alarm, so you drive an Iron Fist punch at his face. His Defence is 7. If you succeed, turn to **262**. If you miss, turn to **272**.

253

There is no rustle or scrape of footsteps on the earth to warn you, nor even the sound of breathing. There is only a rank smell and you stand tensely searching for a sign of the being

that emanates it. The first clue you get is as you are impaled on an invisible horn. Next you are being slashed and clawed from all sides as if by a horde of ravening monsters. Something lifts you off your feet on the end of the horn and you are soon dead. Now it will be the forces of Honoric and those from the Rift which battle for Irsmuncast.

254

Toller of the Spires and the White Mage both state their preference for Doré le Jeune's plan. Glaivas and Gliftel come out in favour of Gwyneth's plan. Then Hickling of Fiendil puts forward his advice. 'We are outnumbered. Therefore our position must be defensive. I counsel a defence using the terrain to best advantage, all across the valley floor. Lady Gwyneth should march now to hold Ruric's Bridge, with her cavalry close behind to plug any gaps should the enemy show signs of breaking through. Two thousand of my footsoldiers and five hundred cavalry should hold the ford, while Gliftel's bowmen occupy Woodnugget Wood. The men of the Spires and their cavalry should form a line from Woodnugget Wood to the Wickerwood close to the ditch. My remaining thousand men and Antocidas' mercenaries should be held in reserve near the Greenridge, where the Overlord should position his command post. Glaivas and his Rangers could hold Colwyn's Mound as back-up. This is my counsel.'

The other Tools and Antocidas come out in favour of this. 'Well, my lord,' says Hengist. 'What is your decision?'

What orders will you issue:

To take up the position advocated by Gwyneth? Turn to **392**.
To take up the position advocated by Doré le Jeune? Turn to **402**.
To take up the position advocated by Hickling? Turn to **412**.

255

From the barren expanse of bare earth that surrounds the Rift you pass into a land of wooded hills and then on into the deepest forest you have ever seen. The tall trees are so close together that they block out almost all the sun's rays, so that you can hardly tell the difference between day and night. These are the Forests of Passing and it is said that those who enter them pass from this world into a twilight realm of dreams and are never seen again. After two – or is it three? – days you come to a clearing where a shaft of sunlight bathes a gaunt figure in a grey robe. You step forwards to ask the way, but the sun passes behind a cloud and when it reappears he is gone and all you can hear is the solemn hooting of an owl. At last, however, the trees thin out and you come to the banks of a beautiful green river. It is the youthful River Greybones, and if you follow its windings it will lead you to the fabled City of Greydawn. Turn to **265**.

256
Your cavalry surges forwards with a triumphant roar, but it runs straight into a volley of crossbow bolts – two thousand cavalrymen fall. It is as if they had run into a brick wall – they are reduced to a tangled mass of men and horses. Suddenly the men between the farm and Tallhill break and run and the Legion comes pouring through. The Greenridge is overrun and you are cut down by a horde of wild legionaries. It is over.

257
By luck alone you cannon into the smoking Imp and knock it to the floor, then drive several blows into its body. If you have the skill of Yubi-Jutsu, Nerve-Striking, turn to **273**. Otherwise the Imp squirms free before you can kill it and it scampers out of the room, still trailing smoke behind it. Turn to **267**.

258
You give the order for a general withdrawal to Bridgebeam. However, you simply do not have enough men to do this. As soon as you give the order, the enemy comes pouring around the flanks and before you know it the orderly retreat has become a full rout. You are killed in the fighting, trying to rally your troops.

259

The message is that a Paladin from Beyond the Rift called Doré le Jeune and four companions, all of whom wear the red cross of Rocheval, Prince of Knights Errant, Wielder of the Holy of Holies, are requesting permission to join your army. You accept and ask Gwyneth to keep an eye on them. Next you call the final war council before leaving the city to march against Honoric.

Turn to **309**.

260

Three winged creatures flap upwards from the area of Manor Ridge. They are Wyverns, vicious creatures of great power. They streak down to attack the men defending the stream, killing them in droves with great bites of their jaws and whipping swings of their poison-barbed tails. This is too much for the men, who break and run in full retreat. The enemy comes pouring through. Many of them swing into the rear of your men at the farm. Soon your whole army breaks into a frenzied rout. As you desperately try to rally your soldiers, you are cut down by a group of heavy cavalry almost incidentally – they do not even know who you are. But, perhaps, you will be remembered in a song, somewhere.

261

'Leave me now. I wish to be alone to think,' you say, and the others file out of Star Chamber. It is vital that you make the right decision. If you wish to consult the scribes for more information about the cities, turn to **61**. If you are ready to make your choice, turn to **281**.

262

A single blow knocks the magician to the ground. He goes out like a light. The sounds of the search are no longer in earshot, and it is a simple matter to make your way out of the camp unseen. You melt away into the night, headed back for the safety of your own forces.

Turn to **100**.

If you have the skill of Yubi-Jutsu, turn to **323**. Otherwise you decide to smash one of the heads between the eyes as hard as you can.

THE SPAWN OF THE RIFT
Defence against Cobra Strike punch: 3
Endurance: 24
Damage: 2 Dice + 3

If you win, turn to **323**. Otherwise your Defence as the three-headed monster tries to bite, gore and impale you is 5 and you cannot block for you must simply try to dodge all of its attacks. If you survive, you may use the Winged Horse kick (turn to **283**), the Forked Lightning kick (turn to **213**) or you may try the Cobra Strike punch again (return to the top of this paragraph).

Your horse prances wildly as the Old One closes in and, leaning out of the saddle, you whip your hand down at its head.

OLD ONE
Defence against Tiger's Paw chop: 7
Endurance: 22
Damage: 1 Die + 2

If you have killed it, turn to **294**. If it still lives, it swings its mace at your ribs. Your Defence is 7. If it hits you, take damage in the normal way and then turn to **304**. If it misses you, will you use the Tiger's Paw chop again (return to the top of this paragraph), spur your horse into it (turn to **284**) or hack at it with your Sceptre (turn to **274**)?

You have rounded the Mountains of Horn, the southern boundary of the Manmarch, while inside the forest, and now you have entered the Lands of Beasts. Men too live here, but their rule is not undisputed. You have little idea what to expect here as you turn a bend in the river and spy a neat patchwork of fields laid out around a city part shrouded in mist. As the day waxes, the mist lifts, to reveal proud gaunt walls built in the style of the ancient Emperors of the Blue Seal: Greydawn is ancient indeed. To your surprise some of the fields are tilled by slaves tied together in rows. Other peasants are obviously serfs, toiling together on the land of their masters. Many are driven on to labour harder by great hog-headed Beastmen, naked to the waist and revealing hugely powerful torsos, their blue-black skin rippling on taut sinews. They pay you scant attention as you approach the city gates. Turn to **275**.

266

The men on the hill charge down its slope and fifteen hundred of the Legion are forced to turn and meet this threat. The mêlée goes on, but now your right flank seems to be holding its own. However, Honoric's cavalry is regrouping behind a screen of crossbowmen.

Suddenly Hengist grabs your shoulder and points to the left. Out of Reekfen Marsh burst the monks of the Scarlet Mantis, some two hundred strong. 'They must have swum down the river unseen from Shadow Forest,' cries Hengist. They dash forwards to assault the left flank of the women of Serakub, who are still bravely holding back Honoric's allies at the ford. But under this new onslaught the women begin to fall back, as many of them have to turn to face the new threat.

Will you order the Elves in Crossway Copse to dart out and attack the monks (turn to **276**) or order the cavalry of Serakub to ride back and attack the monks (turn to **286**)?

267

The Imp's smoke burns your throat as you feel your way through the subterranean passages. You are forced to abandon the chase. When you have passed the tombs of the dead lords and the Imp is nowhere to be found, you pass through the cell that had been used as a Troll's lair and finally out into the graveyard next to the tomb of a long-dead lord, Lord Kalmon. Stealthily you make your way unseen into the dry streets. Turn to **73**.

268

You charge the enemy at the ford and it proves reasonably successful – the men are falling back, but not routed. However, in the meantime your right flank has been overwhelmed and the Legion of the Sword of Doom comes surging through, rolling up your forces. The battle is lost. You try to rally your soldiers, but soon your whole army breaks and runs. You are slain by a group of horsemen, caught in the open trying to rally your men.

269

You return to Irsmuncast in case more troops have arrived to follow your cause. After a day's rest you prepare to march forth once again. At this council of war you must decide how to split your troops. You will need a very strong force to stand a chance of defeating Honoric, but at the same time as soon as you march out to do battle the forces from the Rift will lay siege to the city so you must leave troops behind to defend it. If you stay where you are the enemy forces will unite outside your walls. If, as Gwyneth suggests, you feel that is the most sensible strategy, turn to **199**.

If you march out, then you must select a force which includes at least some native soldiers to remain and protect their home. Lackland, the leader of the troops who were once the Usurper's army, and High Priest at the Temple to Nemesis, suggests that you leave behind the citizen militia and perhaps a thousand followers of Dama to strengthen their backbone. Antocidas scowls at Lackland and says that he recommends leaving Lackland and his 3,500 troops which he values less highly than Gwyneth's 2,000 to strengthen them. The Demagogue urges you to split your forces into two, leaving half to defend the city. Whose advice will you follow, that of Lackland (turn to **279**), Antocidas (turn to **209**) or the Demagogue (turn to **341**)?

You had told the White Mage of what you had seen some hours earlier. Standing nearby, he says quietly, 'My time has come, Overlord,' and then he mutters something inaudible. Suddenly he takes to the air, to the astonishment of all those on Colwyn's Mound, and flies towards the Wickerwood. Just then three winged creatures, the Wyverns, flap up from behind Manor Ridge and streak towards the men of the Spires. The White Mage, high in the sky, his robes glittering in the sun, flies to meet them with bolts of lightning, words of power and potent magic. The Wyverns encircle him, lungeing with their jaws and whipping their poison-barbed tails.

The decimated remains of your cavalry rest nearby awaiting your orders. Then Doré le Jeune gallops up, his armour battered and stained with blood, shouting, 'We must have reinforcements at the stream, Overlord. The men of the Spires cannot hold out much longer!' You look to the left. Honoric's cavalry seems to have pulled back, but the Legion of the Sword of Doom is still trying to break through. However, the wooden walls of the farm and the stout defence of Gwyneth's warriors, the men of Fiendil and Antocidas' mercenaries are holding them at bay. You notice that a thousand men from Fiendil have not yet been committed there. Will you order your cavalry to charge into the fray at the stream (turn to **280**) or order the men at the farm to the stream and keep your cavalry back for now (turn to **290**)?

Lackland is silent. You cannot tell what it is that he wants – perhaps for Honoric to be victorious, even. To your surprise, Solstice has a suggestion: 'Upanishad. It is the largest city on Orb. The largest Temple in the largest city is the Temple to your own Redeeming God, Kwon. It is larger than the rest of his Temples piled on top of one another. The next largest temples there are the Temples to Dama and to Moraine. All of you could have your way.'

'But,' says Hengist, 'Upanishad is beyond the Desert of the Dhervan. At least as far as Wargrave Abbas.'

'There is not time, Solstice,' you comment.

The High Priest of Time looks at you sourly. 'There is always time,' he says, and stalks out of Star Chamber to lock himself inside his Temple once more.

Turn to **261**.

272

The mage stumbles back in horror – luckily for him, as this causes you to miss him. Then he cries out at the top of his voice for aid, fear all over his face. You despatch him quickly, but the searchers have returned within moments. This time there is no escape and soon you are overwhelmed and slain.

273

The Imp utters a high-pitched wail and then dies. The smoke clears slowly and you see that it had been clutching a small potion bottle in its hand. There is no writing on it. It appears in the torchlight to contain a brownish liquid. You may keep it if you wish: note the Vulcan Imp's Potion on your Character Sheet. You make your way quickly through the rest of the dungeon, past the tombs of long-dead lords and past the empty cells, through a room that had been used as a Troll's lair and finally out into the graveyard next to the tomb of a long-dead lord, Lord Kalmon. Stealthily you make your way unseen into the city streets. Turn to **73**.

274

You hack down with your Sceptre. None of your Modifiers apply and you may not use Inner Force. If you hit the Old One, you will do 1 Die + 3 damage.

OLD ONE
Defence against Sceptre: 8
Endurance: 22
Damage: 1 Die + 2

If you have killed it, turn to **294**. If it still lives, it swings its mace at your ribs. Your Defence is 7. If it hits you, take damage in the normal way and then turn to **304**. If it misses you, will you use the Sceptre again (return to the top of this paragraph), spur your horse into it (turn to **284**) or use a Tiger's Paw chop (turn to **264**)?

275

As you are approaching the iron-bound gates they are swung open and an impressive figure rides out at the head of a retinue of lackeys and manservants. He rides a magnificently caparisoned black charger. His hair is braided with cloth of gold and he wears solid gold vambraces studded with diamonds. But the strangest thing is that he is one of the fierce Wolfen, two metres tall and covered in steely grey hairs, while his servants and lackeys are all human. He reins in beside you and gives you a chilling stare. You remind yourself how remarkable you yourself must look in your black costume, albeit tattered from the journey, with your glowing green gem of an eye. He speaks words in a barbaric tongue you haven't a chance of understanding. Will you try to talk to him in the common tongue (turn to **295**) or ignore him and walk on into the city (turn to **325**)?

276

Gliftel and his Elves dash out of the copse and run as fleet as deer. They open fire at the monks as they approach, killing many. Then a skirmish ensues between them, but the pressure on Hivatala's swordsmen is lifted and their withdrawal stops, although they are still struggling to hold their position. If you infiltrated Honoric's camp and found out the contents of three huge wooden boxes, turn to **296**. If you do not know what they contain, turn to **306**.

277

Your offer of aid in the future is greeted derisorily by the followers of Nemesis, and there is further stormy debate during which you realise that you have lost support. One of the older followers of Dama, a bald-headed woman, says that it is highly probable that you will be defeated by the Legion of the Sword of Doom, after which your promise will be as butter in the sun, useless to anyone. The vote goes

against you. Obuda Varhegyen, the head of the Boule, says that you will find no alliance with the people of Serakub. You return forthwith to see to the defence of Irsmuncast, but when Honoric attacks your forces are overwhelmed and you die defending the walls.

278

Glaivas gallops away, his grizzled Rangers behind him. The minutes tick by slowly. Your soldiers at the farm begin to give ground, some legionaries are now among the barn and outhouses. Suddenly several red-robed figures burst from the wood, monks on the run. Glaivas and the Elves, both masters of woodcraft, were too much for them. Within moments a small but accurate hail of arrows goes in the flank of the Legion – any that stray too near the wood tend to get hit. This relieves the pressure considerably, enabling Gwyneth to rotate her warriors in the front line.

'Honoric's cavalry!' someone shouts. Regrouped and ready for another assay, the Bringers of Doom have swung around the farm again. You will have to meet them once more. Raising your Sceptre high, you lead another charge. Make a Fate Roll. If Fate smiles on you, turn to **288**. If Fate turns her back on you, turn to **298**.

279

Lackland's advice proves to be insincere, for in the heat of the battle, when you have met Honoric's forces face to face, his troops turn against you, and Honoric wins a crushing victory. You die trying to take Lackland's life.

280

The cavalry gallops away to crash into Honoric's allies. But then, to your horror, a line of horsemen two thousand strong, headed by the Bringers of Doom clad from head to toe in shining steel, wheel around the flank of the farm and charge hell for leather for the stream. Desperately the reserve swordsmen of Fiendil near the farm try to intercept them, but to no avail. You have no men to stop them, and they drive into the rear of the soldiers at the stream with terrible force. Your warriors are crushed like a nut in a nutcracker. Soon your whole army is in full retreat. Honoric's victory is total. While trying to rally your soldiers you are cut down, almost in passing, by a band of cavalrymen, who do not even know who you are.

281

The time has come for you to announce to your people which city you will seek to make an ally against Honoric, Marshal of the Legion of the Sword of Doom. Will it be Wargrave Abbas (turn to **93**), Greydawn (turn to **103**), the Spires of Foreshadowing (turn to **133**) or Serakub (turn to **183**) or will you visit Solstice at the Temple to Time and ask him to find you time to return from Upanishad and defeat Honoric before he takes Irsmuncast (turn to **153**)?

282

Without changing your stride, you dive forwards and somersault high over the Ogre's head. You are up and running into the night before it even has time to grunt in surprise. There is pursuit, but your mastery of ninjutsu enables you to avoid it with ease, and soon you are running back to the safety of your own forces.

Turn to **100**.

283

There is little point in using finesse against this monster. The Winged Horse kick will do as well as any other, you guess, as you drive your heel at the nearest snapping head with bone-crushing force.

THE SPAWN OF THE RIFT
Defence against Winged Horse kick: 4
Endurance: 24
Damage: 2 Dice + 3

If you win, turn to **323**. Otherwise there is no way that you can block the attacks of all three slashing, goring, snapping heads at once. Your Defence as you leap back and try to dodge is 6. If you survive, you may use the Forked Lightning kick (turn to **213**), the Cobra Strike punch (turn to **263**) or the Winged Horse kick again (return to the top of this paragraph).

284

You try to spur your horse forwards, but it rears back in horror from contact with the strange creature, enabling the Old One to dart in and swing its mace at you. Your Defence is 7. If it hits you, the attack will deal 1 Die + 2 damage and then you must turn to **304**. If it misses you, will you try a Tiger's Paw chop (turn to **264**) or hack at it with your Sceptre (turn to **274**)?

285

The republicans of Serakub do not take to your ugly face and you haven't the charisma to persuade them to be your allies any more. You are forced to leave the city without the promise of support.

Turn to **99**.

286

The horsewomen charge back to assault the monks, which proves effective in driving them back. But in the meantime the Rain of Doom have pulled back, and Honoric's cavalry, some 1,300 strong, has charged Gwyneth's cavalry, alone by the farm. Outnumbered two to one, the cavalry is swept aside by the onslaught, and the Bringers of Doom press on to crash into the right flank of the defenders at the ford. This is too much for them, and they break and run pell-mell. Soon your whole army has been routed. You are caught in the open, trying to rally your troops, by a squadron of the Bringers of Doom and slain out of hand.

287

You have excited them by the thought of striking a blow against the Spawn of the Rift and you are fortunate in that the Boule members become so impassioned and wrapped up in their own oratory that they forget about the allegation levelled against you. You interrupt to say that if you succeed against Honoric you will then turn your powers against the denizens of the Bowels of Orb. Turn to **307**.

288

This time you manage to rout the enemy cavalry completely. A great cheer goes up as the men stream away in headlong flight. Quickly you swing your tired cavalry around into the flank of the Legion. Élite force as it is, even the legionaries cannot hold against such an attack for long. Some of the units break and run, and the rest of the Legion falls back in an orderly fashion. The Doomover Levies also run, despite the swords of the Horngroth.

Soon the whole of Honoric's army is in retreat. You have a victory! Your army gives a joyous shout which gladdens your heart. However, your soldiers are too tired and depleted to pursue and finish Honoric off. Once again he has escaped with his life. Note that you are unable to pursue. Turn to **250**.

289

The enemy is taken by surprise, thinking that the mercenaries were the only force still offering resistance. There is confusion and turmoil in the ranks. The fear of death before the walls were taken has already given way to relief. Thankful to be alive, the Orcs are not prepared to face a new foe. The Dark Elves, however, are made of sterner stuff. The commander, a magnificently accoutred woman with waist-length raven tresses has a blacksteel sword that has already taken the life of Antocidas' second-in-command this night. Will you order Gwyneth to charge the Orcs and see if you can scatter them (turn to **305**) or hurl a shuriken at the commander and then charge the Dark Elves (turn to **319**)?

290

The thousand-strong force sets out at a run to support their comrades at the stream. They arrive just in time to stop a rout – indeed, the enemy is thrown back briefly. Then, to your horror, you see a line of horsemen, with the heavy Cataphracts of the Bringers of Doom shod from head to toe in glowing scaled armour at the centre, thundering towards you from the direction of Tallhill. They have circled around your left flank, driving straight for the back of your warriors at the stream, aiming to crush your men as if between hammer and anvil, the hammer the cavalry and the anvil the Doomover Levies and Honoric's allies. Already the 'anvil' has crossed the ditch and is forcing your men back. They could break at any time. You must act now. Will you order your cavalry to meet the horsemen head on (turn to **240**) or order Doré le Jeune and his Paladins to join you and lead your cavalry personally to meet them head on (turn to **300**)?

291

The throwing star collides with the great spiked club and ricochets harmlessly away, to be picked up by one of the Orcs. You have lost your shuriken and the Troll is closing to do battle. You may use the Leaping Tiger kick (turn to **195**), the Iron Fist punch (turn to **173**) or the Whirlpool throw (turn to **155**).

292

The Ogre roars and tries to smash you with its ham-like fists. You must try to block the blow, and your Defence is 8 for this purpose. If you succeed, turn to **302**. If not, turn to **312**.

293

Shadazar throws her black arms aloft. She is uttering the climactic phrase of the Invocation of Heavenly Wrath as your shuriken buries itself in the back of her brain – cross it off your Character Sheet. She stumbles forwards to the edge of the turret then tumbles over the battlements. She is still able to shriek a curse as she falls to her death, but she is speared upon the banner held by one of her Orcs before the dying curse is finished. You appear at the battlements just as both sides look up to see who has tumbled the commander of the Spawn of the Rift to her death. There is a great moan from the forces of evil, who break and run towards the city gates to the sound of delirious cheering from your citizens. You have delivered Irsmuncast from the forces of evil. Your support from the people will be unwavering if you can govern wisely. Turn to **11**.

294

The Old One lies dead at your horse's feet. You look up to see that the cavalry charge has pressed on and that the Legion is now beating a hasty retreat, in some disorder. You order your men on, to swing around Woodnugget Wood and attack the crossbowmen and then Honoric's allies at the ford. However, at the sight of the Legion falling back, the Doomover Levies on the far left break and flee, despite the swords of the women of Horngroth directly behind them. Realising it is hopeless, Honoric's army begins a general withdrawal. However, your forces are too exhausted to conduct a pursuit. Note that you are unable to pursue. Turn to **250**.

295

You tell the Wolfen that you are Avenger, Overlord of the City of Irsmuncast nigh Edge in the eastern Manmarch. To your surprise the Wolfen seems to understand. He replies that he is Ogg Red-hand, Lord of the mighty Cavalry of Resplendent Empire. His language is the common tongue of a millennium past, all but unrecognisable. You are able to convey to him the reason for your visit to Greydawn, and he says that he will take you to meet the rulers of the city. He seems to believe your improbable story. You cannot tell whether he is cunning or plain stupid, but he looks unpleasantly dangerous. Turn to **335**.

296

You had told the White Mage of what you had seen some hours earlier. Standing nearby, he says quietly, 'My time has come, Overlord,' and then he mutters something inaudible. Suddenly he takes to the air, to the astonishment of all those on the Greenridge, and flies towards Sawdon Freeman's Farm. Just then three winged creatures, the Wyverns, flap up from behind the farm and streak towards Hivatala's soldiers. The White Mage, high in the sky, his robes glittering in the sun, flies to meet them with bolts of lightning, words of power and potent magic. The Wyverns encircle him, lungeing with their jaws and whipping their poison-barbed tails.

Then the crossbowmen of the Legion, the Rain of Doom, begin to fall back, and Honoric's regrouped cavalry prepares to charge Gwyneth and Hivatala's cavalry positioned near the farm and Crossway Copse. Will you order your cavalry to charge in and meet them (turn to **316**) or, taking Doré le Jeune with you, lead your cavalry personally in a counter charge (turn to **326**)?

297

The enemy is taken by surprise, thinking that the mercenaries were the only force still offering resistance. There is confusion and turmoil in the ranks. The fear of death before the walls were taken has already given way to relief that they still live. Thankful to be alive, the Orcs are not prepared to face a new foe. The Dark Elves, however, are made of sterner stuff. The commander, a magnificently accoutred woman with waist-length raven tresses has a blacksteel sword that has already taken the life of Antocidas' second-in-command this night. She shouts orders and then spurs her own horse forwards. She points the sword at the nearest swordswomen and a bolt of purple flame erupts from it, killing several of them instantly. The other Dark Elves meet the charge and the Orcs are rallying. Gwyneth is about to be attacked by the Dark Elf commander. You are some way behind. Will you rush to her aid (turn to **315**) or hurl a shuriken? You may use Inner Force with the shuriken if you wish, but you must decide now (turn to **331**).

298

In the deadly mêlée, you are cut down and trampled to death by a squad of Cataphracts, armoured from head to toe in gleaming scales. So does death come quickly, visiting both beggar and king with equal ease.

299

The Sceptre is secured in a moment and the secret doorway creaks open, revealing rough-hewn steps leading downwards in semi-darkness. The Seneschal finds a torch in a bracket at the stairhead and, striking flint and tinder, sets it alight.

Turn to **329**.

300

Quickly you shout orders and call Doré le Jeune to your side. Up above, the White Mage has slain all the Wyverns, but the price is high. He floats earthwards, his white robes splashed with crimson, his face a contorted mask of pain. He may yet live.

Then, raising your Sceptre high above your head, you cry, 'To battle! For Irsmuncast and freedom for all!' Doré le Jeune shouts, 'For Rocheval!', and the men and women behind you, surging forwards, give a great shout of, 'Avenger!' You are filled with exhilaration as you charge forwards, about a thousand brave warriors at your back. Ahead of you, another line of black-clad horsemen races to meet you.

The impact is shattering as the two lines meet. You find yourself face to face with a Worshipper of Death, a captain of the Wings of Death. You despatch him quickly. Beside you, Doré le Jeune and his Paladins are like a tornado, laying about to terrible effect. What follows is a whirling, running battle that seems to end as suddenly as it began. Honoric's cavalry is retreating fast, though in good order. You have led your cavalry to victory. It was your presence, and that of Doré le Jeune, which gave the men that extra vitality. But they are badly mauled. Some way off, the enemy horsemen, bullied by their officers, are regrouping for another charge. Looking back, you see that your men at the stream have been forced back to Colwyn's Mound. The battle hangs in the balance. Roll a die. If you score a 1, 3 or 6, turn to **310**. If you score 2, 4 or 5, turn to **320**.

301

It has become clear to all present that you must seek an ally, one with a professional army that can be ready to campaign in the Manmarch by the first day of Grimweird. All agree that only you have the charisma to persuade another city to come to your aid. But time is running out. You ask for suggestions as to the best choice of a city for you to visit on a diplomatic mission to enlist the support of another army. Greystaff throws up his hands and says that he knows nothing of armies and war but that his temple will provide healers for the army.

The Demagogue makes the first suggestion: 'Surely there is but one choice, Overlord. The Spires of Foreshadowing have lived under the threat of war from Doomover for all living memory. Their armies have clashed three times this century. With the Tools of Fate on our side we may yet win victory.'

Hengist speaks next: 'The forces of Fate are not our natural allies. At Wargrave Abbas, beyond the Mountains of Vision, we may enlist the aid of the monks of Kwon and the shieldmaidens of Dama, who also have a temple there.'

'Too far,' says Antocidas. 'You could never return from there with an army in time to defeat Honoric. He would be defending our own walls against us.'

Turn to **251**.

302

You leap over its scything arms and dart past the lumbering beast into the night before it even has time to grunt in surprise. There is pursuit, but your mastery of ninjutsu enables you to avoid it with ease, and soon you are running back to the safety of your own forces. Turn to **100**.

303

You call your challenge lustily. Shadazar whirls around, her robe ballooning up to reveal lissom black legs, but she has reached the final phrase of the Invocation of Heavenly Wrath and the bolt of lightning that cracks down from the sky is directed at you. There is nowhere to take cover on the turret, and it reduces you to a blackened husk. Shadazar will be victorious and the eastern Manmarch is lost to man.

304

As the blow connects, you feel a surge of sorcerous energy that emanates from the black glowing mace threatening to engulf you. Make a Fate Roll, but apply −2 to your Fate Modifier for this roll only. If Fate smiles on you, turn to **314**. If Fate turns her back on you, turn to **324**.

305

Gwyneth leads the charge on the Orcs personally. The Dark Elf commander soon divines your intention, however, and spurs her horse towards Gwyneth's. She points her sword and leads a charge of her own against the footsoldiers who form the backbone of your force. The Orcs melt away before Gwyneth's charge, only to re-form and rejoin the fray as soon as she turns to new quarry. The Dark Elf commander's sword belches a gust of purple flame, killing many of the swordswomen instantly. The Dark Elves have woven a powerful enchantment that has caused the chainmail worn by the followers of Dama to grow red hot. The sleeve guards in your own costume have burnt through the cloth and are scarring your arms. You wrestle to cast them to the ground as the main attack comes. Gwyneth has put a hundred Orcs to flight, but your forces are split and defeated piecemeal, many unable to fight due to burns. There is nothing you can do but die honourably, avenging your people.

Three large winged reptilian creatures flap upwards from the vicinity of Sawdon Freeman's Farm. They are Wyverns, fearsome beasts with powerful jaws and poison-barbed tails. They streak down at Hivatala's soldiers to wreak terrible havoc. Within moments the swordswomen break and run. The enemy surges across the ford. As the enemy charges your cavalry near Woodnugget Wood, so Honoric's regrouped cavalry charges there also. Soon your whole army is in full retreat. You are caught in the open, trying to rally your troops, by a squadron of the Bringers of Doom and slain out of hand.

Your words provoke another storm of debate. One of the followers of Dama says that the cause is a noble one and she calls upon the followers of Béatan to vote with them to become your ally. The head of the Boule, a learned man called Obuda Varhegyen, a follower of Béatan, commands rapt attention as he speaks, saying that to become your ally would be to strike a blow against law and that the rule of the war god would bring fatal stagnation and limitation of possibilities. The nature god's followers appear unconcerned, and the followers of Nemesis are against you: one says that to send forces as far away as the Manmarch is to invite attack by the Spawn of the Rift. When the vote is taken, however, it is marginally in your favour. You are asked to a meeting of the Boule leaders immediately after the other items of public business are settled. Turn to **227**.

Doré le Jeune gallops away and leads the cavalry in a full-blooded charge, giving a great battle cry of 'For Rocheval!' Force-Lady Gwyneth leads her Warrior Women in an equally breakneck charge. They catch the enemy cavalry just as it is trying to re-form. There is a sound like thunder as the charge slams home – the whole line of enemy cavalry is physically thrown back, many tumbling into the ditch. Unprepared, the men suffer severe casualties and turn and run immediately. Two thousand crossbowmen step forwards to open fire, but Gwyneth sounds the retreat and your cavalry returns to your lines in good order.

You have won a temporary victory. Although they have lost some men, Honoric's cavalry begins to re-form and the Legion advances once more. Turn to **328**.

309

At last you march to meet Honoric, the man who has done so much to try to encompass your Doom. You have cautioned the Demagogue to watch Lackland like a hawk and to defend the walls staunchly until you return victorious. Unskilled troops are far more useful behind city walls than in the field, but you have chosen to strengthen them also with the many sword-arms remaining of the Usurper's army, and it takes a sizeable superiority in numbers to take a walled city by storm.

You make a fine array of troops, footsoldiers, cavalry, archers, magicians, priests and healers, with as rearguard Glaivas, his Rangers and the Paladins, including Doré le Jeune. After five days' march your scouts tell you that you are nearing Honoric's force, which outnumbers your own. Morale is good and you decide to give battle. You make camp in the valley of the river Fortune and tell your commanders to see that your troops want for nothing and are well rested for tomorrow. The information you have about Honoric's force and its dispositions is fairly meagre. Will you put on an eye-patch to conceal the glowing Orb and do some scouting yourself (turn to **2**) or save your energy and rest well before the battle tomorrow (turn to **342**)?

310

Suddenly there is a great shout of triumph. You look to its source, and you are gripped with despair. Honoric's men have broken into the farm, and Antocidas' mercenaries are retreating in disorder. You lead your cavalry to the farm as quickly as you can, but within seconds the rest of the defenders, attacked in the flank, are fleeing hopelessly. The Legion of the Sword of Doom and the Legion of the Angel of Death surge forward. You meet them head on, but it is not

long before the regrouped cavalry of Doomover slams into your rear, cutting your force to shreds. An unseen sword, thrust into your back, abruptly ends your life.

311

The Sceptre seems to have a life of its own. It is pointing towards the throne. Slowly you walk towards the throne using the Sceptre like a divining rod until the Sceptre's head is resting against the edge of a raised square of marble on the throne, which the hippogriff's head on the throne is also facing. If you have the skill of Picking Locks, Detecting and Disarming traps, turn to **13**. Otherwise turn to **51**.

312

Its fist cracks a rib, and you reel back to lie sprawled on the ground. Already you can hear the sound of approaching guards. You leap up, but by the time you have despatched the Ogre many soldiers have arrived on the scene and you are overwhelmed and slain.

313

Shadazar throws her black arms aloft as you creep stealthily up on her. She is uttering the climactic phrase of the Invocation of Heavenly Wrath. The garrotte wire flexes in your hands as you prepare to strike, but Shadazar suddenly senses your presence. She abandons the spell and whirls to face you, her robe belling up to show lissom black legs. She has time to utter a Word of Power in a language you do not understand before the wire slices into her neck. The wire slices ever deeper, but even as she dies she clutches you to her and you cry out in pain. Her fingers have grown into red-hot pokers which she is driving deep into your vitals. There is a boiling and hissing from inside you, but you try to hang on grimly as your corded muscles drag the wire ever deeper. Lose 9 Endurance. If you are still alive the pain lessens as Shadazar dies and her fingers return to their normal long-nailed form. You stagger back, and her body topples over the battlements to lie sprawled awkwardly on the grass of the Palace gardens. You appear at the battlements just as both sides look up to see who has toppled the commander of the Spawn of the Rift to her death. There is a great moan from the forces of evil, which break and run for the city gates to the sound of delirious cheering from your citizens. You have delivered Irsmuncast from the forces of evil. Your support will be unwavering if you can govern wisely. Turn to **11**.

314

You manage to overthrow whatever magical force threatened you. The Old One growls in frustration. Will you try a Tiger's Paw chop (turn to **264**), hack at it with your Sceptre (turn to **274**) or spur your horse forwards into the Old One (turn to **284**)?

315

You are too late. Gwyneth's horse shies in the face of purple fire spurting from the Dark Elf's sword and she is thrown to the floor and trampled underfoot by the horses of her own swordswomen. The Orcs, recognising her, cheer and, much-heartened, return to the attack. The fight is lost and the only thing you can do is die honourably, avenging the deaths of your citizens.

316

Your cavalry surges forwards and the two forces meet with a resounding crash, the ring of steel on steel. But the heavy cavalry, the Bringers of Doom, the élite of élite, wins the day, and your cavalry is sent reeling back in disarray. The Bringers of Doom press on to crash into the right flank of the defenders at the ford. This is too much for them, and they break and run pell-mell. Soon your whole army has been routed. You are caught in the open, trying to rally your troops, by a squadron of the Bringers of Doom and slain out of hand.

317

The Cave Troll's momentum carries it onwards and you succeed in toppling its balance. Unfortunately it surges powerfully in your grasp and redirects its fall so that you are pinioned on the floor beneath its bulk. It grinds the black spikes of its club into your back. Lose 5 Endurance. If you still live, then at last you succeed in squirming free and you return to the attack more quickly than it can. Will you use a Leaping Tiger kick (turn to **347**), an Iron Fist punch (turn to **337**), or, if you were taught Kwon's Flail in a previous adventure, will you take the opportunity to use this kick (turn to **357**)?

318

Your warriors stand, ready to receive the charge of the Doomover cavalry who, reordered, race at breakneck speed, the sound of their hooves filling the air like thunder. On the left, Glaivas' Rangers ambush the vanguard of Honoric's allies trying to cross the Old Bridge. Fire arrows, pots of Torean fire and guerrilla-like raids by Glaivas' Rangers, hardened warriors, throw them back in surprise and confusion. The Old Bridge goes up in flames. The enemy will have to build some kind of temporary bridge to cross now, under fire from Glaivas and his men as well. The Doomover Levies and the Legion of the Angel of Death are now approaching Crossway Copse.

Honoric's cavalry comes hurtling through and drives into the men of the Spires with a resounding crash, the clash of steel on steel. Your men stagger back, and it looks for a moment as if they will break, but Doré le Jeune is there to rally them and they hold on, just. Then, miraculously, the enemy cavalry is thrown back. The men retire behind the infantry close behind them. Then the five-thousand-strong swordsmen of the Legion utter a bellowing battle-cry and charge forwards into the men of the Spires, who begin to waver under the pressure.

Will you order your reserves forwards to reinforce your struggling soldiers (turn to **358**) or order the cavalry of Irsmuncast and the cavalry of the Spires to charge around in a pincer movement at the flanks of the Legion of the Sword of Doom (turn to **368**)?

319

Gwyneth leads a charge as you pull out your throwing star and the Dark Elf commander points her blacksteel sword straight at her. If you would like to use Inner Force as you hurl the shuriken at the Dark Elf, turn to **349**. If not, turn to **367**.

320

Quickly you survey the battlefield. The men at Hartwig Fell's Farm are still grimly holding on. Will you lead your cavalry back to charge the Doomover Levies and Honoric's allies in the flank (turn to **220**) or pursue the cavalry ahead of you to finish it off (turn to **230**)?

321

Recognising that warriors capable of winning a war for you are not the sort to antagonise, you finish detailing the lands and their proximity to the Rift. Peisistratus and Herris Alchmeonid can see clearly that their 'reward' would be to become your protectors. They frown at each other for a long moment before turning down your offer. Something about their attitude makes you uneasy, but their refusal seems clear enough. Accordingly you decide to try to make Serakub your ally instead, but you will have to run all the way to arrive in time. Turn to **235**.

322

You charge forwards but, at this, so do they. Within moments you have been surrounded and hacked to bits by many men. Your adventure ends here.

323

The grey skin bulges where the three necks meet, high up on the beasts body, as if there were an important nerve centre buried just beneath it. Your Cobra Strike punch hits home and your fingers sink into a surprisingly soft flap of skin. The monster convulses and collapses to the ground at your feet. Though invisible, its pulse can be felt and it weakens gradually and then stops altogether. You decide to leave the corpse for the ants that will detect it by smell alone and continue on your way. This unnatural creature is a creature of the darkness, most likely a pet of the Old Ones, you surmise. Turn to **343**.

324

You feel a cold numbing in your very soul – some part of you has been sucked into the mace. If you have no points of Inner Force left, turn to **334**. Otherwise, lose 1 point of Inner Force. Will you try a Tiger's Paw chop (turn to **264**), hack at the Old One with your Sceptre (turn to **274**) or spur your horse forwards in an attempt to knock the Old One over (turn to **284**)?

325

As you begin to walk past the Wolfen, trying your best to ignore him, the pupils of his eyes narrow to slits most alarmingly and most of his retinue begin the Prayer of the Forgotten Hero, which can mean only that they know he is going to attack you. You duck instinctively as with a blood-curdling howl the Wolfen draws a sword and cleaves the air above your head as if his sword were a natural extension of his arm. He leaps from his horse and presses home the attack ferociously. You are wounded almost to death before the berserk Beastman breathes his last, but his death will avail you nothing. You have killed the commander of Greydawn's cavalry. One of the servants gibbers in terror that you will be impaled if you enter the city. You still have time to retrace your steps to try to win support from the City of Serakub. Turn to **365**.

326

You gallop forwards on your white charger, Doré le Jeune and his Paladins beside you, to take up a position at the head of your cavalry. 'For Irsmuncast and freedom!' you cry, lifting your Sceptre high, as Doré le Jeune shouts, 'For Rocheval!' If you fought the duel with Honoric before the battle, turn to **158**. If you refused to fight, turn to **346**.

327

The huge Cave Troll shakes its great club menacingly as you try to make it strike and miss before dodging in to attempt the Whirlpool throw. Your Defence as you provoke its attack is 7. If it hits you, the black spikes of its heavy brazen club have embedded themselves in your shoulder and you have lost 7 Endurance. Whether it has hit or not you are now close enough to try the Whirlpool throw. So long as you still live, turn to **317**.

328

This time the crossbowmen move in on foot. They are able to re-form much quicker than the cavalry, and the Legion is able to cross over behind the crossbow screen. You dare not unleash your cavalry at them, for they would be cut down in droves. On the left, Glaivas' Rangers ambush the vanguard of Honoric's allies trying to cross the Old Bridge. Fire arrows, pots of Torean fire and guerrilla-like raids by Glaivas' Rangers, hardened warriors, throw them back in surprise and confusion. The Old Bridge goes up in flames. The enemy will have to build some kind of temporary bridge to cross now, under fire from Glaivas and his men as well. The Doomover Levies and the Legion of the Angel of Death are now approaching Crossway Copse.

The crossbowmen fire a volley and then part away to left and right, split into two groups of a thousand men. A great drumming sound fills the air, and Honoric's cavalry comes hurtling through and drives into the men of the Spires with a resounding crash, the clash of steel on steel. Your men stagger back. It looks for a moment as if they will break, but

Doré le Jeune is there to rally them and they hold on. The enemy cavalry, already dismayed by your previous charge, is thrown back again; the men retire behind the infantry. Then the five-thousand-strong swordsmen of the Legion utter a bellowing battle-cry and charge forwards into the men of the Spires, who begin to waver. Quickly you order your reserves, a thousand men of Fiendil, forwards as reinforcements, and the situation stabilises. A bitter stand-up fight to the death is underway. The crossbowmen are guarding the flanks of their infantry – you are itching to send your two cavalry units inwards in a pincer movement, but they would run foul of the Rain of Doom. As this goes on, Hartwig Fell's Farm falls under attack from the Legion of the Angel of Death and the Doomover Levies.

If you infiltrated Honoric's camp last night and discovered the contents of three large wooden boxes, turn to **348**. If you do not know the contents of the boxes, turn to **338**.

329

The Seneschal pulls on the torch bracket and the secret door swings shut behind you. Until the Orcs can fathom its secret you are safe from pursuit. The torch lights a chamber at the bottom of the stairs. The chamber contains a table, arcane tomes and scrolls, and a parchment bearing strange hieroglyphs hangs on one wall. Here it was that you had the misfortune to encounter an Old One, one of the nameless horrors of the deepest catacombs of the Rift. The Seneschal reaches for one of the scrolls and unfurls it, but you caution him that there is no time to lose. 'But, Overlord, these may be magical scrolls of use against the despoilers of our city.'

A red glow creeps around the walls. The Seneschal screams, drops the scroll and looks at the spot where it falls as if it were a viper. His body jerks and he falls to the floor. The torch goes flying and all is lost in darkness. Even the night vision of an owl is to no avail here in the Palace dungeons. By the time you have found the torch and nursed lit back into flame the Seneschal is already dead. The back of his skull has been laid open to reveal the pulpy morass of his mangled brains. There is the faintest sound of something approaching and you steel yourself, waiting for your unseen foe to attack. Will you turn around suddenly in case the thing that killed the Seneschal is going to attack the back of your head as well (turn to **137**) or remain facing the fallen body (turn to **181**)?

330

You jump high into a somersault, drawing shouts of approval from your own lines and surprising Honoric completely. He wheels to face you but you lash out with incredible speed, a Winged Horse kick that sends him staggering back. Note that he has lost 5 from his Endurance of 24. He growls in anger and pain. Turn to **350**.

331

The shuriken is whizzing through the air just as the Dark Elf commander is pointing her sword at Gwyneth. If you used Inner Force to hurl it at the Dark Elf, turn to **349**. If not, turn to **367**.

332

At this, one of them says, 'There's an intruder in the camp, some filthy spy of that lily-livered so-called king of Irsmuncast, no doubt. Line up here. We've been delegated to find him, and you can help us!'

'About time you Aveneg lot did something,' says another, which causes a ripple of laughter nearby. You join the ranks of men who are searching for you. It is an easy matter to slip away behind as they comb the camp, and it is not long before you are running through the night towards your own troops, laughing to yourself at the stupidity of the men of Doomover. Turn to **100**.

333

The throwing star has buried itself in the Troll's face. It staggers but does not go down. Its vision is impaired, however, and you may increase your Defence by 2 during your battle with the grey warted Troll. It is also wounded.

Roll one die and subtract the result from the Cave Troll's Endurance of 20. The Orcs cower back in fear as you attack. Will you use the Leaping Tiger kick (turn to **195**), the Iron Fist punch (turn to **173**) or the Whirlpool throw (turn to **155**), or, if you were taught Kwon's Flail in a previous adventure, will you use the opportunity to open with this kick (turn to **211**)?

334

All your will and volition have been drained from you. You are now a zombie under the control of the Old One. It forces you to order a general retreat before you are taken back to Doomover as an object of ridicule, an amusing entertainment, before you are finally executed.

335

Ogg escorts you through the streets and squares of Greydawn, each of which boasts an equestrian statue of Moraine, the God of Empire, majestic and arrogant. Ogg tells you that some of the statues are three thousand or more years old. As you pass a blackstone temple that is built in the shape of the whirlpool of Nemesis, the Supreme Principle of Evil, Ogg Red-hand makes obeisance, describing the shape of a whirlpool on his forehead. The sight of the Wolfen doing this seems strangely bizarre, and it makes your flesh creep. At last you stand before the most magnificent temple you have ever seen. Great columns rise up in row after row towards mosaic roofs of lapis lazuli and gold-leaf somehow inured to the weather. Another shining golden statue to the God of Empire stands astride the enormous stairway that leads to the temple gates. Inside you meet two whom Ogg says are rulers of this strange city. Turn to **395**.

336

When Honoric sees your approach, he shouts an order and out of the Manor House comes a small force of Orcs, Ogres and Dark Elves. Doré le Jeune instantly cries, 'Riftspawn!' and charges to attack, forcing you to order your men to charge behind him. While you are engaging them, Honoric and his remaining troops make good their escape. Soon your superior force has routed the creatures of the Rift, but your warriors cannot go on to pursue Honoric. However, his army will not be a threat to the Manmarch for years to come. Tiredly you set about the task of setting your weary army's footsteps on the road to Irsmuncast, still threatened by the creatures of the Rift. Turn to **420**.

337

The Cave Troll has begun whirling its great brass club around its head, hoping to sweep you off your feet when the club hits home. The club's black spikes whistle menacingly through the air as you dart in to deliver a straight punch to its midriff.

CAVE TROLL
Defence against Iron Fist punch: 5
Endurance: 20
Damage: 2 Dice + 1

If you have defeated the Cave Troll, turn to **411**. Otherwise the club is whistling towards your own midriff. You try to leap high above it. Your Defence is 8. If you are still alive you may try the Leaping Tiger kick (turn to **347**), the Whirlpool throw (turn to **327**) or punch again (return to the top of this paragraph).

338

Then three winged creatures flap upwards from the area of Manor Ridge. They are Wyverns, vicious creatures of great power. They streak down to attack the men of the Spires defending the line from the farm to Colwyn's Mound, killing the men in droves with great bites of their jaws and whipping swings of their poison-barbed tails. This is too much for the men, who break and run in full retreat. The enemy comes pouring through. Many men swing to the rear of your men at the farm. Soon your whole army breaks into a frenzied rout. As you desperately try to rally your soldiers, you are cut down by a group of heavy cavalry almost incidentally. They do not even know who you are. But, perhaps, you will be remembered in a song, somewhere.

339

Shadazar's purple robes billow in the breeze as she invokes another bolt of lightning from the heavens. She has her back to you and is intent upon her spell, only five metres away. Will you creep up behind her and use your garrotte (turn to **313**), hurl a shuriken at the back of her head (turn to **293**) or call out to her in the hope that this will put her off her spell (turn to **303**)?

340

You jump to meet him. You manage to grab his wrist, but when you try to throw him you find that his strength is such that you cannot move him. He whips his arm across in a great buffeting blow and you are flung back. Lose 2 Endurance. Turn to **350**.

341

The Demagogue knows little of the ways of war and in following his advice you have made a bad mistake. Dividing your forces in two leaves you too weak to defeat Honoric, who inflicts a crushing loss on your army. You are killed while rallying some of your troops, who are being pursued from the field.

342

Dawn breaks. Examine the map on the next page. Currently your army is encamped along the Greenridge and Tallhill. As the sun rises you can see a stream of village refugees hurrying over the Old Bridge and down the road. The reason is obvious. Sprawled around the Manor House is the army of Honoric, the leader of the Legion of the Sword of Doom, their lines stretching from Sawdon Freeman's Farm to Squire's Hill. Your scouts, Glaivas' Rangers, are out at the stream, as are the scouts of the Legion. Soon they will return with news. You begin issuing orders to bring all your commanders together for a council on this portentous day.

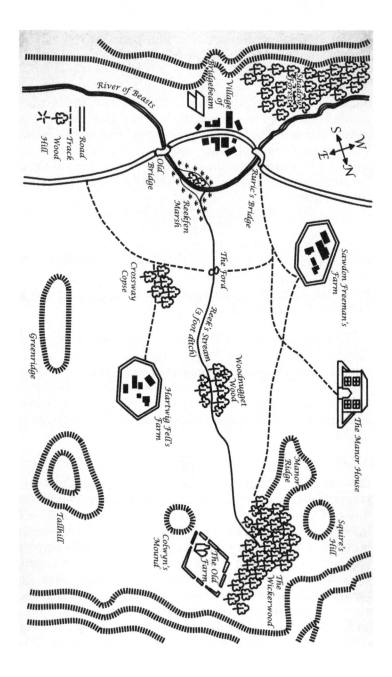

If your allies are the men of Fate from the Spires and Fiendil, turn to **352**. If they are the worshippers of Moraine from Greydawn, turn to **362**. If they are the warriors of Béatan and Dama from Serakub and Aveneg, turn to **372**.

343

You have not gone much further when a new threat presents itself. Three giant crows, each large enough to bear a man, carry three figures towards you. Your excellent vision, not of the green world of the planes as seen through the Orb, for these are natural beings, allows you to tell at a distance that they are Dark Elves, probably spellcasters, for they carry only short stabbing swords and wear no armour. You decide to take a stand between a gaunt tree that has been struck by lightning, and a pier of naked rock. The crows glide clumsily to the ground and the Elf riders dismount at three corners of a triangle of which you form the centre. Each wears a strange purple headdress with a bloated green spider perched on top. They are instantly recognisable as worshippers of Nullaq, 'She who rules in malicious envy'. Each places a small purple executioner spider on the ground before them. The spiders are no bigger than a man's thumbnail, yet their bite kills a horse in seconds. Each casts a spell upon the spiders and then all three chant musically in unison your name, Avenger. You have been named as the one the spiders must attack. Turn to **373**.

344

Doré le Jeune gives a joyous shout and spurs his horse forwards. A great rippling roar goes up from your cavalry and the men pound forwards, hell for leather, looking fearsome with their swords high in the air and glittering in the sunlight. The footsoldiers surge forward, soon outdistanced by the cavalry. It is a magnificent sight. However, they have trouble crossing the ditch, and the crossbowmen, the Rain of Doom, step forwards with military precision and unleash a volley of bolts with crippling accuracy. The cavalry re-forms and charges onward again at full gallop. But there are more crossbowmen than cavalrymen in any case, and they are the best crossbowmen in the Manmarch. Volley after volley crashes into them. Rank after rank go down as if they had ridden into a stone wall. The carnage is terrible to behold. Within seconds your cavalry has been decimated. None reaches the enemy. They simply break and turn tail, streaming past the infantry, which stops and wavers, uncertain, as the cavalry flees. However, the Elves have been pouring a withering fire into the flanks of the enemy, nearest the wood, who are edging away.

Suddenly the crossbowmen of Doomover, with drill-like movements, hurry aside to enter the wood in an attempt to flush out the Elves. Behind them, the legions of the Spires and Aveneg, the women of Horngroth, the men of Mortavalon and the Doomover Levies utter a throaty roar and charge forwards – eight thousand men rushing in a mass, a frightening sight.

Will you order your men to stand their ground (turn to **374**) or order them to try and fall back to the stream in good order, to take their original positions and there make a stand (turn to **384**)? In any case you have little choice but to try personally to rally your retreating cavalry, so you mount your charger and ride off to intercept it.

345

The bolt of lightning causes one of the horses to rear and buck. The horse catches its hoof in a flowerpot and lands heavily on top of you. One of the Trolls is quick enough to tread on your head, squashing it, before you can squirm from beneath the stricken animal. Shadazar will be victorious now and the eastern Manmarch is lost to man.

346

There is silence behind you as you and your cavalry charge forwards. Despite the Sceptre you sense that the men have lost confidence in you. As you draw closer to the enemy, the Bringers of Doom raise their swords high. For the first time you notice that many of them have black glowing blades. It becomes clear that they have a similar effect to Honoric's sword Sorcerak, for fear radiates from them like a wave of nauseous horror. The two sides come together with a resounding crash, the clash of steel on steel. Abruptly, amid the whirling mêlée, a well-aimed sword thrust takes you in the eye, driving the Orb back into your brain, and you are killed instantly.

347

The Cave Troll waves its great brass club. The black spikes are already dripping with blood, which it wishes to mix with your own. As it strikes cumbersomely you launch yourself into the air and drive the heel of your foot at its chest. Unfortunately, the Troll's reach is long and you may be caught by the spiked club.

CAVE TROLL
Defence against Leaping Tiger kick: 7
Endurance: 20
Damage: 2 Dice

If you have defeated the Cave Troll, turn to **411**. Otherwise it tries to sweep your legs out from under you with a cunningly low-angled swipe of its spiked club. Your Defence is 6. If you survive, you may counter attack with another kick (return to the top of this paragraph), an Iron Fist punch (turn to **337**) or a Whirlpool throw (turn to **327**).

348

You had told the White Mage of what you had seen some hours earlier. Standing nearby, he says quietly, 'My time has come, Overlord,' and then he mutters something inaudible. Suddenly he takes to the air, to the astonishment of all those on Tallhill, and flies towards the Wickerwood. Just then three winged creatures, the Wyverns, flap up from behind Manor Ridge and streak towards the men of the Spires. The White Mage, high in the sky, his robes glittering in the sun, flies to meet them with bolts of lightning, words of power and potent magic The Wyverns encircle him, lunging with their jaws and whipping their poison-barbed tails.

Quickly you survey the scene. On the far left, the enemy has managed to extend a wooden raft-like bridge out across the river. Glaivas is still keeping the enemy back, a remarkable feat, but it will not be long before the men are across. The pressure is mounting on Hartwig Fell's Farm, where the Legion of the Angel of Death is taking heavy losses but simply keeps on coming – it is as if the Legion had no fear of death at all, and losses are mounting among the defenders. The Doomover Levies are attacking in a desultory half-hearted manner.

On the right, a vicious struggle is going on as the Legion increases the pressure all the time, its cavalry now joining the throng assaulting the cavalry of Irsmuncast, near Hartwig Fell's Farm. The presence in the Wickerwood of the Eves has turned out to be vital. A messenger arrives, explaining that the monks of the Scarlet Mantis have been trying to penetrate the Wickerwood to fall on the Old Farm, and that a deadly game of cat and mouse is going on in the wood between the two equally matched sides.

The battle is reaching a critical point. Will you order Antocidas' mercenaries to wheel to the left and attack the crossbowmen on the Legion's flank (turn to **398**) or order your whole left flank to swing up into the Doomover Levies, the Warrior Women of Horngroth and the Legion of the Angel of Death (turn to **418**)?

349

The Dark Elf senses rather than sees the shuriken cleaving through the air towards her and she brings up her blacksteel blade to parry. Her skill is great. The blade meets the spinning star with a clash, but the force of Kwon the Redeemer is behind the five-pointed steel. There is a grinding noise as of some infernal engine and the blacksteel blade shatters, covering her embossed armour in shards. There is a wail from the Orcs, for the sword was their talisman of invincibility. Gwyneth's sword claims the unarmed commander's life, and the battle turns against your enemies, who soon break and run towards the city gates. Antocidas, a burly scar-faced veteran, strides out of the barracks courtyard where he had been fighting, kneels and beseeches you to lead him on to victory. Gwyneth gives the order to advance upon the Palace. Cross the shuriken off your Character Sheet and turn to **375**.

350

You circle each other warily. Honoric's features are a mask of concentration, the concentration of a master swordsman. Will you try a Forked Lightning kick (turn to **360**), an Iron Fist punch (turn to **370**) or a Teeth of the Tiger throw (turn to **380**)?

351

As Solstice had said, it is generally held that Upanishad is the largest city on Orb, with more than a million souls. It is also called by some the City of the Redeemer because the followers of Kwon there are so powerful. It caters for as many creeds as Goth of Ten Temples, however, and twice as many species. The most powerful man in the city is reputed to be the Grandmaster of the Stars, whom people call the Right Hand of the Redeemer, but he seldom leaves the Duomo monastery. Upanishad lies between the deltas of the Great and Khesh rivers north of the Jungle of Khesh. It is a hundred days' journey. Even a sea raid on Doomover from Upanishad could hardly take place before the month of Pantheos, by which time Honoric would have taken Irsmuncast in your absence unless Solstice can find you more time. Return to **61**.

352

A large trestle table has been erected. You sit at its head, the Sceptre in one hand. Around the table sit Force-Lady Gwyneth, the four Tools of Fate – Happening, Kelmic, Hoitekh, and Toller – the commander of the force from the Spires, General Hickling of Fiendil, Glaivas the Ranger, Captain Gliftel of the Sundial Elves, the White Mage, Hengist the Grandmaster, Doré le Jeune the Paladin, and Antocidas the One-Eyed. Turn to **124**.

353

Cold panic grips you as you feel your flesh knitting around the Orb, which is soon firmly embedded in your eye socket. The emerald presses in, causing a sudden pain in your head, but this soon passes. Running your hands over your face you can feel that it has taken position just as if it were a translucent green eyeball. The severed muscles of your old eyeball regrow until you are surprised to realise that the green Orb moves in your head just as your real eye does. Then the whole world turns a ghostly green. You are seeing through the Orb. Opening one eye at a time allows you to see a normal world or a green world of ghostly planes and visions which are superimposed on reality. Note on your Character Sheet that you see through the Orb of Kings, and if you have played Book 4: *OVERLORD!* then restore your lost Modifiers.

There is the sound of uncouth orcish voices on the staircase below. Will you leap down to do battle (turn to **233**) or, if you have the skill of Climbing, climb down the outside of the Palace tower to the smoke-obscured gardens below (turn to **247**)?

354

The men of Fiendil charge forwards at your signal, uttering a guttural war-cry. They catch the cavalry unawares, but the Bringers of Doom, armoured from head to toe and the finest cavalry in the Manmarch, have regrouped and are able to fend off your charge with a counter charge. Then the Legion of the Sword of Doom, who reorganised themselves as if they were on a parade-ground and not a battlefield, pour around the flanks of your army. Your men are on open ground, outnumbered three or four to one. Within moments they have been surrounded and annihilated. You can do nothing but watch the horrible carnage.

You have lost the battle before it has begun. Honoric orders a general attack, and your position is assaulted from all sides. There are simply not enough men to hold the left flank, and in a matter of minutes it is swept away. Soon your whole army is routed. You are slain by a group of Cataphracts as you try to stem the tide of your fleeing men, almost out of hand – they do not even know who you are.

355

The bolt of lightning causes one of the horses to rear and buck. It catches its hoof in a flowerpot that breaks beneath it, and you use the cover of the prancing stallion to reach the Palace gates. You are past the startled Dark Elves who guard it before they know you are there, and you race on up the stairs to the battlemented tower. The only enemies you meet are Orcs who have found the Palace wine cellars and are now too drunk to hinder you. Soon you are at the top of the staircase. Turn to **339**.

356

You spur your mounted troops on for another charge. Sensing victory, they cheer wildly. You catch the enemy cavalry trying to re-form; demoralised and disordered, they are not up to another assault. They break and flee in complete disorder. Keeping a tight rein on your cavalry's desire to go after them you wheel them around and charge hell for leather into the back of the Legion of the Sword of Doom. Caught unawares, the legionaries scatter and run. At this, Honoric orders a general withdrawal and his men begin to retire in the direction of the Manor House. Your cavalry is still reasonably intact, Gwyneth's infantry on the far left is virtually still fresh. Note that you are able to carry out a pursuit. Turn to **250**.

357

The Cave Troll brandishes a great brass club with black spikes as it lumbers to the attack. The Seneschal backs away, afraid. You wait as if paralysed with fear for the Cave Troll to strike then you whirl your body and lash out with the devastatingly powerful Kwon's Flail kick.

CAVE TROLL
Defence against Kwon's Flail kick: 6
Endurance: 20
Damage: 2 Dice

If you have defeated the Cave Troll, turn to **411**. Otherwise the Troll is trying to smash you with its spiked club. Your Defence is 5 as you dodge nimbly aside. If you survive the attack, you cannot practically use Kwon's Flail again in such quarters and may counter with a Leaping Tiger kick (turn to **347**), an Iron Fist punch (turn to **337**) or a Whirlpool throw (turn to **327**).

358

Quickly you order your reserves, a thousand men of Fiendil, forwards as reinforcements, and the situation stabilises. A bitter stand-up fight to the death is under way. The crossbowmen are guarding the flanks of their infantry. You are itching to send your two cavalry units inwards in a pincer movement, but they would run foul of the Rain of Doom. As this goes on, Hartwig Fell's Farm falls under attack from the Legion of the Angel of Death and the Doomover Levies.

If you infiltrated Honoric's camp last night and discovered the contents of three large wooden boxes, turn to **348**. If you do not know the contents of the boxes, turn to **338**.

359

The great grey warted Troll lumbers cumbersomely forwards. It is about as broad as the doors to the Throne Room. The Orcs cower back, eager to see you smashed to a pulp without exposing themselves to danger. The Troll sneers horribly at you. Will you use the Leaping Tiger kick (turn to **195**), the Iron Fist punch (turn to **173**) or the Whirlpool throw (turn to **155**), or, if you were taught Kwon's Flail in a previous adventure, will you use the opportunity to open with this kick (turn to **211**)?

360

As you close in, Honoric slashes at your head, but you lean back and then drive your foot at his knee and then up to his throat. If you succeed and you have the skill of Yubi-Jutsu, you may add 2 to the damage, but you may not combine Nerve-Striking with Inner Force.

HONORIC
Defence against Forked Lightning kick: 9
Endurance: 24
Damage: 1 Die + 5

If you have reduced Honoric to 6 or less Endurance, turn to **390**. If Honoric is not yet seriously wounded, his sorcerous blade speeds towards your abdomen. Your Defence is 7. If you are still alive, will you try another Forked Lightning kick (return to the top of this paragraph), an Iron Fist punch (turn to **370**) or a Teeth of the Tiger throw (turn to **380**)?

361

You look to Gwyneth next for her suggestions. 'Return to the city of your forefathers, Avenger, Serakub Beyond the Rift. I am sure you could persuade Hivatala the Swordsmistress of the Guard at the Temple to Dama there to ride to our aid.' Turn to **271**.

362

Unfortunately, you were doomed from the moment you allied with Greydawn. You position your forces in a sound practical way, but as soon as the battle starts the men of Greydawn march away to the left to join up with the thousand men of Mortavalon who also worship Moraine, Ogg Red-hand laughing wildly as he gallops away. The worshippers wait for the outcome of the battle, probably intending to attack the winner, of which there can be no doubt. You are outnumbered six to one, and Antocidas is already leading his men off the field. Honoric sounds a charge, and although you fight desperately your pitiful force is crushed and you are cut down. It is over.

363

Battle is joined with the fearsome Trolls, though they take a heavy toll. You have just felled one that a shieldmaiden on your left starts to torch when there is a great crack in the sky. Shadazar has called down a bolt of lightning from the heavens which has not killed her Trolls but has turned you into a charred husk. Victory is hers and the eastern Manmarch is lost to man.

364

Roll a die. If you score 5 or 6, turn to **394**. If you score 1 to 4 turn to **10**.

365

Your wounds and the strain of making up time as you force your way through the Forests of Passing take a terrible toll, for there is no time to find a healer without falling into the clutches of those who would avenge the Wolfen. Apply −1 to your Punch, Kick, and Throw Modifiers, as your body is permanently weakened. But at last you are south of the Rift once more. Turn to **235**.

366

You lead your victorious troops to crash into the flank of the Legion. The Legion staggers back in disarray and begins to break up. However, you had not properly dealt with the enemy cavalry. Regrouped, it charges back into the fray, and your cavalry is crushed between forces of the Legion of the Sword of Doom. An unseen sword thrust in the back abruptly ends your life. Perhaps you will be remembered in a song.

367

The Dark Elf senses rather than sees the shuriken cleaving through the air towards her and she brings up her blacksteel blade to parry. Her skill is great. The blade meets the spinning star with a clash and the shuriken shatters harmlessly upon her embossed armour. All you can do is rush to Gwyneth's aid. Turn to **315**.

368

The cavalry leaps forwards with a battle-cry, but it has to pass across the front of the crossbowmen on either side of the Legion. Two devastating volleys of bolts hit the cavalry at close range, and before your very eyes your cavalry is a struggling mass of writhing men and horses, as if they had ridden straight into a stone wall. The few survivors have fled in terror. At the sight of this, the footsoldiers of the Spires break and run, allowing the Legion of the Sword of Doom to sweep around and roll up your forces completely. Soon your whole army is on the run. Pursuit and slaughter ensues. You are cut down by a squad of the Bringers of Doom as you desperately try to rally your forces. The horsemen do not even know who you are. Perhaps you will be remembered in a song some day.

369

Your return to Irsmuncast is celebrated with feasting, and the mood of the people is lifted when the news of your alliance with Dom the Prescient is spread abroad. Messengers and envoys asking for help have been sent to many places, but no-one has yet joined your banner. Rumours that Honoric is on the march reach you, and you double the scouting patrols out to the west and also east towards the Rift. It is still possible that your worst fears may be correct, that the Spawn of the Rift are waiting for a chance to strike as Honoric does. The city defences have been repaired and your troops are drilling daily, though the rabble militia will never make an effective fighting force in time.

At last your scouts bring news of friendly troops approaching. The next day the streets are lined with cheering people as the four Tools of Fate, Hoitekh, Kelmic, Toller and Happening, lead a magnificent force of three thousand foot soldiers and the five hundred Cavalry of the Wheel into the city. They wear particoloured surcoats in the four colours, blue, green, red and yellow, to symbolise the coats of many colours that their priests wear. Indeed, Hoitekh and Happening are wearing full dress robes of many colours which, together with the coloured standards of their men, are a riot of colour. Two days later, similar scenes are re-enacted as General Hickling from Fiendil, the city north of Irsmuncast, leads another three thousand men into the city and another five hundred medium cavalry. At last you have a fighting chance. Note your allies are the Spires of Foreshadowing and Fiendil, then turn to **159**.

370

You try to drive your fist into his face as he slashes at you with Sorcerak. If you succeed and you have the skill of Yubi-Jutsu, you may add 2 to the damage, but you may not combine Nerve-Striking with Inner Force.

HONORIC
Defence against Iron Fist punch: 8
Endurance: 24
Damage: 1 Die + 5

If you have reduced Honoric to 6 or less Endurance, turn to **390**. If Honoric is not yet seriously wounded, his sorcerous blade speeds towards your throat. Your Defence is 7. If you are still alive, will you try a Forked Lighting kick (turn to **360**), another Iron Fist punch (return to the top of this paragraph) or a Teeth of the Tiger throw (turn to **380**)?

371

Battle is soon joined with the fearsome Trolls, and they begin to take a heavy toll. You manage to slip unchecked behind them when there is a great crack in the sky. Shadazar has called down a bolt of lightning from the heavens which has not killed her Trolls but has turned some of the mercenaries and shieldmaidens into charred husks. Make a Fate Roll. If Fate smiles on you, turn to **355**. If Fate turns her back on you, turn to **345**.

372

A large trestle table has been erected. You sit at its head, the Sceptre in one hand. Around the table sit Force-Lady Gwyneth, Doré le Jeune, the White Mage, Antocidas the One-Eyed, Swordsmistress Hivatala, commander of the women of Serakub, Obuda Varhegyen, commander of the men of Béatan from Serakub, the High Priest Ba'al, commander of the men of Béatan from Aveneg, Gliftel, captain of the Elves of Sundial, Glaivas and Hengist, the Grandmaster of Kwon. Turn to **238**.

373

All around the rock and the tree is bare burnt earth. The spiders can scuttle quickly across the ground and it is unlikely that you can escape from the triangle for you will be bitten. If you have training in Immunity to Poisons, turn to **215**. Otherwise, will you try to kill them at a distance with your throwing stars (turn to **383**), hurl a shuriken at one of the Dark Elves (turn to **403**), climb the tree (turn to **413**), use the skill of Feigning Death, if you have it, behind the pier of rock (turn to **5**) or advance towards one of the spiders, keeping the rock and the tree between you and the other two (turn to **15**)?

374

The men of the Spires resolutely take a defensive posture, but they are out in the open without the benefit of the terrain. The horde of howling swordsmen crash into them with a resounding crash that echoes across the battlefield.

To your horror, within moments they have been swept away, and the enemy comes pouring through. The monks of the Scarlet Mantis burst out of the Old Farm, where they had crept unheard from the Wickerwood, and assault Colwyn's Mound. There are two hundred of them, and all your nearest troops are routed. You put up a strong defence, but it is not long before you are overwhelmed and slain.

375

The din of pillage rolls unabated, but Gwyneth holds your troops to their purpose and soon you are marching up Palace Road. The forces from the Rift are taken by surprise. Soon you have gained the Palace gardens, while many of the Orcs and Dark Elves have been put to flight. As you are about to triumphantly make your entrance, Gwyneth draws your attention to a figure staring down with hatred from the battlemented tower. It is the commander-in-chief of the forces from the Rift, Shadazar, a Dark Elf whom you recognise from her likeness in the Tome of Maledictions in the Palace library. She gathers her purple robe about her and begins to cast a spell. If you have a Vulcan Imp's Potion and would like to drink it now, turn to **399**. If you do not have a potion or prefer not to drink it since it could be poison, you may consider concocting a plan (turn to **389**).

376

You and Doré le Jeune charge into battle once more with two hundred of your bravest warriors behind you. You surround the creature, but your weapons seem to have no effect on it whatsoever. Even Doré le Jeune cannot dent its steely hide. But the Colossus lays about itself with its great sword, killing a score of men with one blow. Two strikes of its sword and you and your men are fleeing back. At the sight of this your forces begin a spontaneous withdrawal. If you were able to pursue Honoric's defeated army earlier, note that you are now not able to do so. Turn to **386**.

377

'Who would believe the word of a trickster?' cries a follower of Nemesis. The followers of Dama turn away from you. Only the followers of Béatan seem unperturbed, and one argues that the facts remain as they are stated. But the vote goes heavily against you. Obuda Varhegyen, the head of the Boule, says that you will find no alliance with the people of Serakub. You return forthwith to see to the defence of Irsmuncast, but when Honoric attacks your forces are overwhelmed and you die defending the walls.

378

Your soldiers fall back in good order, taking up their former positions just in time to receive the charge of Honoric's allies, whose first assault is beaten off. But they renew the attack and a desperate struggle begins. Your whole army is under attack, save the cavalry on Colwyn's Mound and the mercenaries at the Old Farm. You have no option left to try to save the battle other than to order Antocidas to take his mercenaries and charge the crossbowmen on the flank of the Legion of the Sword of Doom. Turn to **26**.

379

The shuriken is hurtling towards the Troll's warted face long before it even realises what is happening. Make an Attack Roll. The Troll's Defence is only 4. If you succeed, turn to **333**. If you fail, turn to **291**.

380

You leap up and try to twist your feet around Honoric's head, but he is much too quick and experienced a warrior to allow himself to be caught out. He ducks and cuts at your calves with Sorcerak. Lose 1 Die + 5 Endurance. If you still live, the burning blade fills you with agony. Will you use a Forked Lightning kick (turn to **360**) or an Iron Fist punch (turn to **370**)?

381

Very little is known about Greydawn, a city often literally shrouded in mist at sunup. It lies south of the Rift and west of the Great Plateau. The only other cities in the same valley of the River Greybones are the City of the Runes of Doom and the Walls of Shadow, both cities of the dead. It was once a civilised city from where a large empire was ruled, but that was long ago. The Temple to Moraine is thought to dominate the city, but the scribes find a reference to a Temple to Nemesis and to Beastmen. It may well be that the followers of Moraine wish to have an empire again and the only way they can expand is northwards into the Manmarch. Return to **61**.

382

You invite suggestions from your commanders. Refer to the map at **342** as needed.

Gwyneth suggests a defensive formation with a refused left flank. 'The right flank should rest on the Wickerwood, with Gliftel's Elves in the wood itself. Antocidas' mercenaries can hold the Old Farm, with some cavalry positioned on Colwyn's Mound, and then a line of units stretching to the Greenridge, with the centre resting in Hartwig Fell's Farm. A thousand men could be held in reserve on Tallhill, where the Overlord Avenger's command post should be. Finally, I would suggest that Glaivas and his Rangers should wait in ambush at the Old Bridge to hold it for as long as possible should any try to cross it.'

Doré le Jeune leaps up and says: 'No, no. We should attack, though we are outnumbered! Take the fight to

Honoric and his black-hearted lackeys! Put all our cavalry and three thousand of our best footmen before the stream between Woodnugget Wood and the Wickerwood. Gliftel's fine bowmen could occupy Woodnugget Wood, to give flanking fire as I and my comrades personally lead the charge to drive through to the open ground beyond Manor Ridge, whence we can strike back to the ford or on to the Manor. The rest of our army should hold Hartwig Fell's Farm in case of a flank attack from across the ford. The Overlord's council post should be on Colwyn's Mound, from where Avenger can give support to the attack, along with the White Mage of Avatar.'

At this point Doré le Jeune bows respectfully to the old magician. Turn to **254**.

383

The spiders scuttle quickly across the burnt earth towards you, zig-zagging and darting wildly. They seem to gravitate towards cracks in the ground and stones automatically as if in search of safety. Note how many throwing stars you have and then roll a single die to see how good your marksmanship is. Add the die score to the number of shuriken you have left. If the total is 1 to 6, turn to **35**; 7 to 9 turn to **65**; or 10 to 11, turn to **85**.

384

You give the order. They respond to the signal with alacrity and begin to give ground steadily, in good order, but the enemy is approaching fast. Roll one die. If you score a 5 or a 6, turn to **20**. If you score a 1 to 4, turn to **30**.

385

A great grey-skinned Cave Troll, three metres tall, rounds the corner and stands uncertainly before you. The Orcs all point at you and say 'enemy', whereupon the Troll's face cracks open in a horrible grin and it begins twirling around its head a huge brazen club with black spikes. If you would like to wipe the smile from its face using a shuriken, turn to **379**. Otherwise you must depend upon the martial arts skills of the Way of the Tiger (turn to **359**).

386

As the Colossus closes in, Gliftel, whom you are pleased to see still lives, runs fleetly to meet it with three of his fellows. They stop some seven metres ahead of it and begin to murmur and move their hands in complicated patterns in the air, casting some spell. The ground before the Colossus shifts and it steps forwards, not on to firm fields of grass but on to a huge boggy patch of quicksand. It sinks to its chest and begins to flail about. Gliftel says a word and the earth hardens, leaving even a Colossus hopelessly trapped. Gliftel and his companions run back, laughing gleefully. You cannot help but smile, and Doré le Jeune, battered and wounded as he is, is roaring with mirth.

Are you still able to conduct pursuit? If so, turn to **396**. If not, turn to **406**.

387

Hivatala had estimated that it would take her perhaps a tenday longer than you to reach Irsmuncast with her army. 'Gwyneth will be overjoyed to see you at the head of your troops,' you had told her, but as you skirt the Bowels of Orb you all but run into a warband of Orcs almost a thousand strong. In avoiding them, you catch sight of another even larger warband marching to join it. The signs suggest that you may suffer another attack from the Spawn of the Rift before too long. You only hope that Hivatala manages to win through with her army intact.

Turn to **409**.

388

If you went on a mission to scout out Honoric's camp, came across three large boxes and managed to discover their contents, turn to **44**. Otherwise turn to **54**.

389

While you pause to consider what to do, five great Cave Trolls lumber out of the Palace gates to spearhead a counter attack. Will you lead a charge against them (turn to **363**) or slip past them and try to get inside the Palace (turn to **371**)?

390

Your last blow sends Honoric sprawling backwards gasping in pain. Shouts of joy and anger rise up from the warriors on either side. Desperately he points at you with his sword and rasps, 'Fly, Sorcerak!' The sword shoots from his hand straight at you. If you have the skill of Arrow Cutting, you are able to deflect the rune-etched blade. Otherwise it cashes your shoulder and you lose 4 Endurance. If you still live, Sorcerak spins in the air and hurtles back to its master's outstretched hand. Turn to **8**.

391

Serakub, the city of your forefathers, is also called the City of Gardens. It is larger even than the Spires of Foreshadowing, with perhaps as many souls sheltering inside its walls. The scribes say that it is hard to understand their version of the common tongue. The largest temples there are to Dama, Béatan the Free, a god who despises law and order but who is not evil, and to Ilexkuneion, a strange nature god whose priests call themselves druids. The followers of Dama patrol the lands between the city and the Rift. They hate the Spawn of the Rift more than all else. It lies a tenday beyond the Bowels of Orb. Return to **61**.

392

Gwyneth smiles. 'Victory may yet be ours, Overlord,' she says, and she rides away to organise the disposition of the troops.

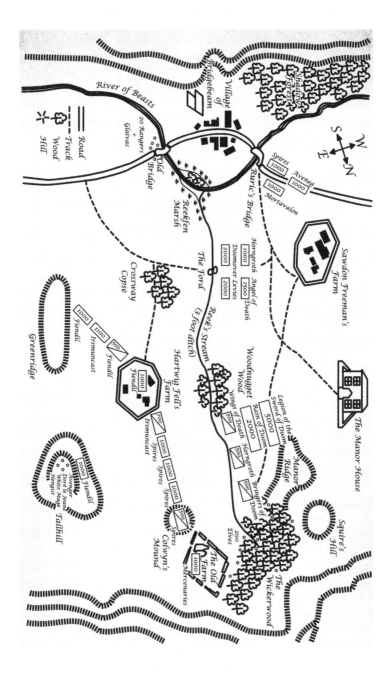

Doré le Jeune and the White Mage decide to stay with you on Tallhill to await events before committing themselves. So do Hengist and his comrades. As your men move into position, so Honoric reacts. His dispositions are shown on the map on the previous page. Note this paragraph number down as a record of your strategy and so that you can refer to the map when the battle begins. Turn to **388**.

393

You sprint back up to the Palace roof and peer over the edge of the battlements to the gardens below. The smoke thins to reveal a sea of brutish Orc faces looking up expectantly. There is no escape that way, so you descend the stairs once more. The Orcs have lined up in the hallway behind a great grey-skinned Cave Troll, three metres tall, who had been about to climb the stairs after you when you reappeared. It sneers horribly, shaking a huge brazen club with black spikes. There is no time to think. Will you use the Leaping Tiger kick (turn to **195**), the Iron Fist punch (turn to **173**) or the Whirlpool throw (turn to **155**)?

394

You notice that Doré le Jeune is annoyed by this order. In fact, he rides across the front of the cavalry, his sword high, shouting something. Then he and his Paladins charge towards the enemy. A great rippling roar goes up from your cavalry and the men surge forwards, hell for leather, looking fearsome with their swords high in the air and glittering in the sunlight. You curse Doré le Jeune under your breath as you helplessly watch the three thousand footsoldiers of the Spires hurtle after them, caught up in the spirit of the charge. It is a magnificent sight, although you had not wished for it. However, they have trouble crossing the ditch, and the crossbowmen, the Rain of Doom, step forwards with military precision and unleash a volley of bolts with crippling accuracy. The cavalry re-forms and charges onwards again at full gallop. But there are more crossbowmen than cavalrymen in any case, and they are the best crossbowmen in the Manmarch. Volley after volley crashes into them. Rank after rank go down as if they had ridden into a stone wall. The carnage is terrible to behold. Within seconds your cavalry has been decimated. None reaches the enemy. They simply break and turn tail, streaming past the infantry, which stops and wavers, uncertain, as the cavalry flees. However, the Elves have been pouring a withering fire into the flanks of the enemy, nearest the wood, who are edging away.

Suddenly the crossbowmen of Doomover, with drill-like movements, hurry aside to enter the wood in an attempt to flush out the Elves. Behind them the legions of the Spires and Aveneg, the women of Horngroth, the men of Mortavalon and the Doomover Levies utter a throaty roar and charge forwards – eight thousand men rushing in a mass, a frightening sight.

Will you order your men to stand their ground (turn to **374**) or order them to try and fall back to the stream in good order, to take their original positions and there make a stand (turn to **384**)? In any case you have little choice but to try personally to rally your retreating cavalry, so you mount your charger and ride off to intercept it.

395

The two rulers to whom Ogg introduces you could not be less alike. One is a great ox of a man with a ruddy complexion and the tan and callouses of a man used to sword practice in the sun. The other has the olive-green pallor of one who shuns the sun. He is tall and almost unnaturally thin, as though he suffered from a wasting disease. Strangest of all, however, is the fact that seven spherical gems of different colours hover above his head and move with his movements as if attached to him by invisible wires. Both are dressed in the gold and azure finery of Moraine.

When you talk of war you can sense their interest. Nobody would ever attack them in this backwater region. Their nearest neighbour is the Fleshless King of the City of the Runes of Doom. They have nowhere to use their military might. Yet Peisistratus, the thin one, says that there will be no reward for their defeating your enemies. Remembering the words of Antocidas, you offer them a large tract of land which you refer to as 'Barren Lands'. They fall in with your plan surprisingly quickly and invite you to review their troops. You can hardly believe how well things are going and wonder whether the Sceptre holds power even when you do not invoke it. If you have the skill of ShinRen, turn to **129**. If you have not, and decide to tell the truth about the perils of the 'Barren Lands' and, most likely, be forced to look to Serakub for help, turn to **321**. If you brave it out in Greydawn, turn to **415**.

396
'Come.' says Doré le Jeune. 'The day's work is not yet done. We must make sure Honoric's defeat is complete, and most of all try to slay that black-hearted villain.' Will you order a pursuit (turn to **416**) or decide to head for home (turn to **406**)?

397
After a while you realise you are being followed by an innocent-looking old scribe wearing the pale blue robes of the scholars' guild. When you turn away from the great cathedral towards the Palace of Dom the Prescient, ruler of the city, the scribe quickens his pace surprisingly, and you wait warily for him to catch you up at the steps to the Palace gates beyond the huge stables. He rips off his robe and shows you the mark of the four-handed God of Assassins, Torremalku the Slayer. 'Fear not, stranger, if you have nothing to fear. I serve His Highness whose Palace it seems you wish to visit. Now declare your business within the city. These are troubled times.' Will you tell him your mission (turn to **407**) or say that you have come to seek work in the Palace kitchens (turn to **9**)?

398
Before you give the order your attention is drawn to the left flank. You see, galloping back towards you, Glaivas with perhaps ten Rangers left. Behind him come three thousand footsoldiers streaming over the River of Beasts and headed

for the men of Fiendil and the Women Warriors of your city on your extreme left flank.

They receive the charge of Honoric's allies, whose first assault is beaten off. But they renew the attack and a desperate struggle begins. Your whole army is under attack, save the cavalry on Colwyn's Mound and the mercenaries at the Old Farm. You have no option left to try to save the battle other than to order Antocidas to take his mercenaries and charge the crossbowmen on the flank of the Legion of the Sword of Doom. Turn to **26**.

399

The potion tastes of molasses but has an acrid tang. As soon as it enters your stomach you feel as if you are on fire inside, then as if your flesh were melting. Next, visions come and go of strange animals and beasts. First a hippogriff, then a snail, then a roaring bull. Unless you can concentrate on one, you feel you will go mad. The snail seems to come most easily. Will you concentrate on that (turn to **125**), the roaring bull (turn to **117**) or the hippogriff (turn to **109**)?

400

You lead your men in a charge in pursuit of Honoric. After a time, he and perhaps a thousand legionaries still under arms, die-hard veterans, turn at bay, unable to flee any longer. The battle is short and bitter, every one of them fighting to the last man. You see no sign of Honoric in the fight as you battle on, but at the end Doré le Jeune brings you his body, inert and lifeless, the once powerful limbs still, the arrogant, always angered face calm and relaxed in death. 'How harmless he seems now,' says the Paladin. 'No longer shall he terrorise the weak and innocent. Of his sword, Sorcerak, there is no sign.'

So, at last, it is over. Doomover will not threaten the Manmarch for years to come. Tiredly you set about the task of setting your weary army's footsteps on the road to Irsmuncast, still threatened by the creatures of the Rift. Turn to **420**.

The Spires of Foreshadowing, even larger than Doomover and Irsmuncast, is the largest city in the Manmarch. The spires that give the city its name are awesome to the newcomer. It is a city that is full of life and of many different types of people, ruled over by Dom the Prescient and the followers of the goddess Fate. There is also a temple to the war god Vasch-Ro, He who sows for the Reaper, and the followers of Fate see Doomover and the followers of Vasch-Ro as their greatest enemy. The Tools of Fate, heroes who, it is said, have been singled out by the Keeper of the Balance herself, reside there and command the famous Cavalry of the Wheel. The Spires of Foreshadowing lies between Irsmuncast and Doomover, slightly nearer to the latter. It is a journey of two tendays away. Return to **61**.

Doré le Jeune leaps up and shouts, 'Victory to the righteous! We shall ride forth and smite the evil in this world wherever we find it! To battle!' And he rides off to organise the troops, with a parting: 'I await your orders, Overlord!'

The White Mage, Glaivas and his Rangers, and Hengist with his comrades decide to stay with you on Colwyn's Mound to await events before committing themselves. As your men move into position, so Honoric reacts. His dispositions are shown on the map opposite. Note this paragraph number down as a record of your strategy and so that you can refer to the map when the battle begins.

Turn to **388**.

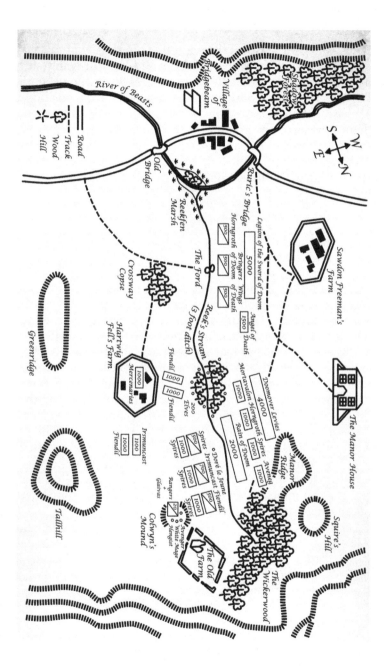

Road
Track
Wood
Hill

River of Beasts

Village of Bridgebeam

Shadow Forest

S W N E

Old Bridge

Ruric's Bridge

Reekfen Marsh

Sawdon Freeman's Farm

Horngroth of Doom | 500
Bringers of Death | 500
Wings of Death | 500

Legion of the Sword of Doom
5000

The Ford (3 foot ditch)

Reek's Stream

Angel of Death | 1500

Crossway Copse

Hartwig Fell's Farm

Doomover Levies
4000

The Manor House

Greenridge

Mortavalon Horngroth Spires | 1000 | 1000 | 1000

1000 Mercenaries

Fiendil | 1000
Fiendil | 1000

200 Elves

Rain of Doom | 2000

Spires | 500
Irysmuncast | 1000
Fiendil

Manor Ridge

Ebryn's Avenel | 1000

Squire's Hill

Irysmuncast | 1100
Fiendil

Irysmuncast Spires | 750
Fiendil

Doré la Jeune | 1000
Spires

Spires | 1000

Talhill

Rangers + Giarvas

Cofwyn's Mound

Avenger White Mage

Spires | 200
Spires | 1000

Hengist

The Old Farm

The Wickerwood

403

Your shuriken flashes through the air, but your target breathes a spell of transmutation and the throwing star becomes a feather that flutters harmlessly to the ground. With a shock you realise you have lost sight of the positions of two of the spiders. You look around warily, but one of them crawls under a stone nearby and, as you step back towards it, rushes out and sinks tiny fangs in your heel. The poison courses through your veins and death is swift. Now Honoric and the forces from the Rift will carve up the fate of Irsmuncast.

404

Honoric, a great bull of a man in black-studded chainmail, rides up to the ditch opposite and glares at you. 'So we meet again, Avenger, you lily-livered lackey of Kwon, the Babbler of Half-Truths.' He dismounts as do you. 'This time I will kill you,' he says through gritted teeth. His hatred for you is almost tangible. He draws his sword, Sorcerak, with a flourish. The black, smoking blade emanates an evil aura and you are riven with fear. To throw off its effects you must expend a point of Inner Force; otherwise the horror you feel affects your ability to fight. Apply –1 to all your Modifiers for this combat only. Honoric bellows angrily and leaps over the ditch towards you, swinging his sword. A cheer goes up from the serried ranks of his army. If you have the skill of Acrobatics and wish to try jumping high and somersaulting over his charge to land behind him, turn to **330**. Otherwise you can leap forwards to meet him and try a Whirlpool throw as he comes down (turn to **340**) or you can jump back out of range (turn to **350**).

405

You hear no more from Radziwil. He is reported dead soon after. One of his guards of Warrior Women has been over-zealous. Now, there are no more Orcs or others to give your position away as you change direction. Turn to **37**.

406

Honoric leaves the field of battle. His army will not be a threat to the Manmarch for years to come. Tiredly you set about the task of setting your weary army's footsteps on the road to Irsmuncast, still threatened by the creatures of the Rift. Turn to **420**.

407

The assassin tells you to wait in a side chamber of the Palace. You never see him again, but a page boy comes to invite you into the presence of 'Dom the Prescient, he who sees all things that are to come to pass'. As you walk through the final hallway before that in which Dom the Prescient sits in state, the page boy indicates a pedestal and says: 'That is where the bodyguard Everyman stood for three centuries until he disappeared mysteriously last year.' At last you are entering the royal presence. Turn to **29**.

408

Unfortunately they do not make it back to the safety of secure terrain and are caught in the open. It is not long before their flank is enveloped and a slaughter begins, outnumbered almost three to one as they are. Your forces break and run in a full rout. It is not long before the rest of your army follows as your whole left flank is rolled up. You are caught in the open, trying to rally your men, and slain by a squadron of the Bringers of Doom, who cut you down almost in passing. They do not even know who you are.

409

Your return to Irsmuncast is celebrated with feasting, and the mood of the people is lifted when the news of your alliance with the republic of Serakub is spread abroad.

Messengers and envoys asking for help have been sent to many places, but no-one has yet joined your banner. Rumours that Honoric is on the march reach you, and you double the scouting patrols out to the west and also east towards the Rift. It is still possible that your worst fears may be correct, that the Spawn of the Rift are waiting for a chance to strike as Honoric does. The city defences have been repaired, and your troops are drilling daily, though the rabble militia will never make an effective fighting force in time.

At last your scouts bring news of friendly troops approaching. The next day the streets are lined with cheering people as Hivatala, Swordsmistress of the Guard at Serakub, leads into the city a force as large as she had promised: two and a half thousand foot soldiers, shieldmaidens and reverencers of Béatan, and five hundred cavalry whose horsemanship is a joy to behold. Four days later another force arrives of two thousand from Aveneg, six hundred of whom are the illustrious Cavalry of Myriad Possibility, and similar scenes of jubilation are re-enacted. The shieldmaidens fit in well with Gwyneth's troops in their grey, white and green, with the shield of Dama blazoned everywhere, while the followers of Béatan look equally splendid in their yellow surcoats. At last you have a fighting chance. Note your allies are Serakub and Aveneg, then turn to **159**.

410

Then Hivatala stands and speaks, her accent outlandish and strange even having heard her before. You are barely able to understand her. She suggests refusing the right flank, with Gwyneth's swordswomen holding Ruric's Bridge. Her own troops would hold the ford, with all the cavalry of Dama on their right up to Hartwig Fell's Farm. Antocidas' mercenaries would hold the farm, with the rest of the troops in a line to Tallhill, which would be occupied by a thousand men. Four hundred men of Béatan could be held in reserve, with the Elves occupying Crossway Copse. Your command post would be on the Greenridge.

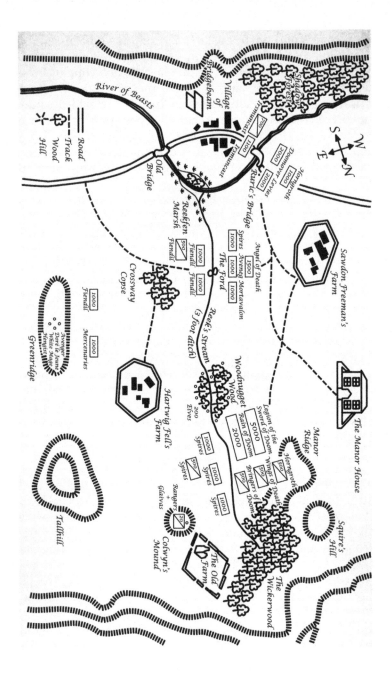

Antocidas and the White Mage favour this counsel. Glaivas and Gliftel come out in favour of Gwyneth's advice. Ba'al and Doré le Jeune favour the counsel of Obuda Varhegyen.

What orders will you issue:

To take up the position advocated by Gwyneth (turn to **14**)?
To take up the position advocated by Obuda Varhegyen (turn to **24**)?
To take up the position advocated by Hivatala (turn to **34**)?

411

The Troll's body smashes to the floor and you whirl to face the Orcs in the doorway. They draw back, unwilling to attack one whom they have just seen slay a Cave Troll. One of them, fatter than the rest and wearing a makeshift iron crown, calls for crossbows. It seems they intend to pepper you with quarrels from the safe distance of the doorway. The Seneschal calls you to follow him. He is passing his hand up and down the wall behind the throne. 'Quickly, Overlord. The beast is coming back to life.' Your own flesh crawls as you see the Troll's tattered flesh stretching and crawling across the bones to reknit itself. The wounds are disappearing before your very eyes. In this case, you decide, discretion is the better part of valour and you hasten to join the Seneschal. The secret doorway creaks open, revealing rough-hewn steps leading down into semi-darkness. The Seneschal finds a torch in a bracket at the stairhead and, striking flint and tinder, sets it alight. Turn to **329**.

412

General Hickling nods with grim satisfaction. 'So shall the blade of Honoric be blunted on the shield of our defence,' says Happening, portentously.

Doré le Jeune and the White Mage decide to stay with you on the Greenridge to await events before committing themselves. So do Hengist and his comrades. As your men move into position, so Honoric reacts. His dispositions are shown on the map opposite. Note this paragraph number down as a record of your strategy and so that you can refer to the map when the battle begins. Turn to **388**.

413

Quickly you climb the tree, but the three spiders arrive at different sides of the dead trunk simultaneously and they scurry up the pale bark with undiminished speed. You try to squash them with the sides of your hands, but they all leap upwards on to your outstretched hands at the last moment. Tiny fangs pierce your skin and poison courses through your veins. Death is swift. Now Honoric and the forces of the Rift will carve out the fate of Irsmuncast between them.

414

You ride forward on your white stallion and shout: 'I accept your challenge, Honoric!' A great roar comes from your troops. They have great confidence in their ninja-lord in single combat. Honoric, his three-horned helmet and studded armour looking too heavy for any normal man to carry, rides forth, his own troops also shouting frenziedly. Honoric rides to the ditch between Woodnugget Wood and the Wickerwood and you ride to join him. The duel is on, and it will probably decide the battle. Without you, your force will disintegrate. Turn to **404**.

415

The soldier lord of Greydawn, Herris Alchmeonid, and Ogg Red-hand are justifiably proud of their army. They drill with great precision and, resplendent in their gold and blue, the troops look every bit a match for even the Legion of the Sword of Doom. There is an élite corps of Wolfen, called the Wolf Warriors, legions of the powerful Beastmen and other legions of men. Peisistratus explains how Alchmeonid is in charge of four legions, each a thousand strong, two of men and two of Beastmen. Ogg will command the Cavalry of Resplendent Empire and the Wolf Warriors. They will be ready to march within days and will follow you on to Irsmuncast to where you return forthwith in order to look to its defence until their arrival. Turn to **419**.

You gather together those warriors still able to continue, some three thousand cavalry and footsoldiers, and set out in hot pursuit of Honoric's scattered forces. You cross the ford and march on towards the Manor House. Honoric is still trying desperately to rally some of his men. Did you manage to stop any of the Orcs, Ogres and Dark Elves from the Rift getting past you in the vicinity of Irsmuncast? If you prevented reinforcements from the Rift, turn to **400**. If six hundred creatures of the Rift managed to get past you, turn to **336**.

The city is strangely calm as you march into Palace Road. As the gates of the Palace come into view, you realise that you have lost the element of surprise. Radziwil's advice has led you into a trap. The Orcs are no longer looting. The commander-in-chief of the forces from the Rift, Shadazar, a Dark Elf enchantress of great power whom you recognise from a likeness in the Tome of Maledictions in the Palace library, stands majestic in purple robes atop the Palace battlements and begins to orchestrate your ruin. Five Cave Trolls advance stolidly, and the Orcs are forced to the attack by Dark Elves. There are too few of you to survive the onslaught. All you can do is sell your life dearly avenging your subjects.

The cavalry of Fiendil and the footwarriors of Irsmuncast and Fiendil charge forwards. The Doomover Levies turn to face them. For a moment it looks as if your men will sweep them away, but those Levies that break and run are cut down by the women of Horngroth who stand behind them. They withstand your attack and a mêlée ensues.

Then to your left you see, galloping back towards you, Glaivas with perhaps ten Rangers left. Behind him come three thousand footsoldiers streaming over the River of Beasts and headed for the now exposed flank of the men of Fiendil and the Women Warriors of your city. They will be upon them in moments. Your troops have no option but to fall back. Desperately they give ground, but the Women Warriors of Horngroth charge forwards to try to turn the withdrawal into a rout. Roll 1 die. If you score 1, 3 or 5, turn to **378**. If you score 2, 4 or 6 turn to **408**.

419

Your return to Irsmuncast is celebrated with feasting, and the mood of the people is lifted when the news of your alliance with the forces of Greydawn is spread abroad. Messengers and envoys asking for help have been sent to many places, but no-one has yet joined your banner. Rumours that Honoric is on the march reach you, and you double the scouting patrols out to the west and also east towards the Rift. It is still possible that your worst fears may be correct, that the Spawn of the Rift are waiting for a chance to strike as Honoric does. The city defences have been repaired and your troops are drilling daily, though the rabble militia will never make an effective fighting force in time.

At last your scouts bring news of friendly troops approaching. The next day the streets are lined with cheering people as Herris Alchmeonid, the general in command of the Greydawn forces, leads a magnificent battle array into the city. First there are two thousand followers of Moraine in glistening gold and deep blue, the colours of their God of Empire. Their old-fashioned golden breastplates blaze in the sunlight. The crowd goes a little quiet when the next two and a half thousand troops march in. These are the Beastmen, and a truly ferocious fighting force they look, bare to the chest with mighty sinews rippling beneath their blue-black skin. By the time Ogg Red-hand the Wolfen rides past at the head of the Wolf Warriors and five hundred cavalry, the crowd has overcome its surprise and cheers twice as hard. At last you have a fighting chance. Note your ally is Greydawn, then turn to **159**.

420

The journey takes many days, but finally you are near the City of Irsmuncast. An ominous pillar of dark smoke reaches up to the sky on the horizon. Gwyneth is looking worried as a murmur of disquiet goes up from the soldiers. Quickly you lead a forced march to reach the city as soon as possible.

When you do reach it, an army ten thousand strong, mostly of Orcs and Goblins from the Rift, surrounds Irsmuncast. Parts of the wall are aflame, but the city has not yet been sacked. It seems you have arrived just in time. You begin to prepare for another battle, but at the sight of you and your army the forces of the Rift begin to pack up their camp and march away, the Orcs snuffling and growling as they run along.

You enter the city in triumph, hailed as a hero. 'The saviour of Irsmuncast,' the common people call you. But what trials await you next, now that you have defeated Honoric of Doomover?

Continued in the Way of the Tiger 6: INFERNO!

If you enjoyed *Warbringer!* then you may like to try these other classic adventure gamebooks from Fabled Lands Publishing.

More details and free game resources at:

www.sparkfurnace.com/collections

FABLED LANDS

A sweeping fantasy role-playing campaign in gamebook form

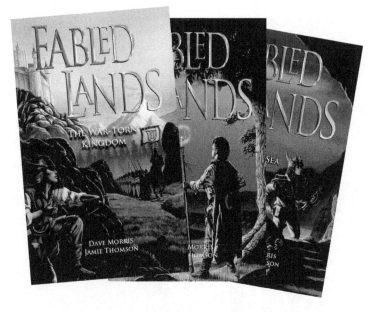

Set out on a journey of unlimited adventure!

FABLED LANDS is an epic interactive gamebook series with the scope of a massively multiplayer game world. You can choose to be an explorer, merchant, priest, scholar or soldier of fortune. You can buy a ship or a townhouse, join a temple, undertake desperate adventures in the wilderness or embroil yourself in court intrigues and the sudden violence of city backstreets. You can undertake missions that will earn you allies and enemies, or you can remain a free agent. With thousands of numbered sections to explore, the choices are all yours.

The return of BLOOD SWORD —
the groundbreaking multiplayer gamebook series
created by Dave Morris and Oliver Johnson.

Blood Sword can be played either solo or in a
team of up to four people, combining the best of
role-playing, gamebooks, and boardgames.

WAY OF THE TIGER Collectors' Edition

Megara Entertainment have limited stocks of the full-color Way of the Tiger hardcovers.

megara-entertainment.com

Made in the USA
Las Vegas, NV
27 December 2020

14844648R00132